QUEEN
VICTORIA'S
BUCKINGHAM
PALACE

QUEEN VICTORIA'S BUCKINGHAM PALACE

Amanda Foreman and Lucy Peter

Royal Collection Trust

Introduction

There is no more recognisable symbol of the British monarchy than Buckingham Palace. Since 1837 the Palace has performed a unique function as the private London home of the royal family, the administrative headquarters of the monarchy and the symbolic centre for the spirit of the nation. In good times and bad the famous East Front balcony has formed the backdrop to some of the most memorable scenes in history.

The Buckingham Palace of the twenty-first century is the result of many alterations and enlargements. Yet in its purpose and essence the Palace remains the creation of Queen Victoria and Prince Albert. When the Queen moved into the Palace in 1837 it had been unoccupied for almost 20 years. George IV had lavished vast sums of money on it but the work remained incomplete by the time he died in 1830. William IV had no interest in finishing the project and even tried to give the Palace away. Victoria inherited a home that was unmodernised and badly planned. What she needed was a building that harmoniously combined three separate roles into one: public, private and state. What she had was a historical mish-mash of rooms from three different reigns: the entertaining and public spaces were far too small, the kitchens antiquated, the private apartments wholly inadequate for a family, and the plumbing and heating almost non-existent. Addressing the Palace's problems was a daunting prospect but at the same time it was also a marvellous opportunity to create something new and modern that would be in tune with the rapid changes taking place in British society.

Victoria and Albert's designs for Buckingham Palace were a labour of love. They regarded the Palace as a reflection of their moral values and belief in the importance of family life (Fig. 1). The way they entertained demonstrated their combined sense of purpose. Art and music were shared passions, and they invited many of the most esteemed musicians and composers of the day to perform at the Palace. Between 1840 and 1861 the Palace was transformed into one of the most glittering courts in Europe.

The death of Prince Albert on 14 December 1861 almost put a stop to the achievements of the previous 21 years. Queen Victoria could not bring herself to live in Buckingham Palace during her long widowhood. Incapacitated by her grief, she not only abandoned the Palace but also her public role as Sovereign. Without an occupant or even a purpose, Buckingham Palace became a painful reminder to the public of a glorious era cruelly cut short. The story of Victoria's eventual return to public life is revealed in the slow but sure rejuvenation of the Palace. There were some things that the Queen could never bear to resume there because they intruded too much on personal memories: she never again attended a concert, or played host to a visiting head of state, or gave a ball like the magnificent ones of old. But, with the help of her Prime Minister, Benjamin Disraeli, Victoria developed other ways of opening Buckingham Palace to the wider world. One of the most visible is the invention of the summer garden party, which began in the 1860s and became a regular feature thereafter.

Fig. 1
Queen Victoria and Prince Albert portrayed with five of their children in 1846

By the end of Queen Victoria's life, Buckingham Palace had returned to its place at the heart of the nation. The Palace had a starring role in Victoria's Golden and Diamond Jubilees in 1887 and 1897 respectively, serving as a physical and emotional focus for the celebrations surrounding her 60-year reign. Her death in 1901 marked the end of an era, but Victoria's Palace and the traditions she instituted endure to this day.

A New Beginning

For Victoria, Buckingham Palace not only marked the beginning of her new life as Queen but her own personal freedom from the oppressive governance of her mother and the restrictions that Kensington Palace, her childhood home, represented.

Victoria, christened Alexandrina Victoria and known to everyone as Drina, was born at Kensington Palace on 24 May 1819. As the only legitimate surviving grandchild of George III, at birth Victoria was fifth in the line of succession, shortly behind her father, Edward, Duke of Kent, and her three much older uncles, George, the Prince Regent (later George IV), Frederick, Duke of York, and William, Duke of Clarence (later William IV).

In early 1820, when Victoria was only eight months old, tragedy struck. Victoria's father died of pneumonia, leaving Victoria's mother, the Duchess, alone to raise her infant daughter (Figs 2 and 3). Alongside Sir John Conroy, the Comptroller of the Duchess's household, Victoria's mother imposed a strict and controlling set of rules on her daughter, which came to be known as the 'Kensington System'.

As well as providing Victoria with a highly structured formal education, the Kensington System also dictated that she could only play with a very select number of hand-picked playmates and was not allowed to be in the company of anyone without a third person present. Added to this, until her accession, Victoria had to share a bedroom with her mother and, for several years, was forbidden from walking downstairs without someone holding her hand. Although the Duchess clearly loved Victoria, as surviving letters show, Victoria's childhood was stifling and lonely, with the future Queen spending much of her time surrounded by adults, in particular her governess, Baroness Louise Lehzen (Fig. 4), with whom she created 132 dolls during the early 1830s (Fig. 5). Much later, Victoria described her years at Kensington in a letter to her own daughter, concluding 'I had led a very unhappy life as a child – never had a father – and did not know what a happy domestic life was!'.

ABOVE
Fig. 2
This painting of the Duchess of Kent was presented to Victoria by her mother on the Princess's fifteenth birthday

RIGHT
Fig. 3
An early portrait of Princess Victoria and her mother, the Duchess of Kent. The Duchess is shown in mourning for her late husband, the Duke of Kent, and Victoria is holding a miniature of him

Fig. 4
Sketch by Princess Victoria of her governess, Baroness Louise Lehzen, with the Princess's pet dog, Dash, seated to her left

However, that was about to change. At just after 2am on 20 June 1837, Victoria's uncle, William IV, died. Only three hours later, the Archbishop of Canterbury, accompanied by Lord Conyngham (the Lord Chamberlain), arrived at Kensington Palace to inform Victoria – who received the two men while still in her dressing gown – of her accession (Fig. 6). Given Victoria's childhood experiences, it is perhaps unsurprising that the first thing she did on receiving the news was request an hour alone and that her bed be moved out of her mother's bedroom. Within just three weeks, all of Victoria's possessions had been packed up and she was on her way to Buckingham Palace.

Queen Victoria, accompanied by her mother, arrived at Buckingham Palace on 13 July 1837. With the Dowager Queen Adelaide still residing at Windsor Castle, and her Aunt Augusta living at Clarence House, Buckingham Palace was the most logical choice for the new Queen.

A watercolour from 1846 shows the Palace as it looked on Victoria's arrival (Fig. 7). The horseshoe-shaped design – a central building with two wings extending eastwards, flanking an imposing triumphal arch – was the vision of two men: George IV and his architect, John Nash. When George III died in 1820 his son and heir, George IV, quickly set about transforming his mother's unimposing London town house (Fig. 8) into a palace. The work took more than ten years, went vastly over-budget and remained uncompleted when George IV died in 1830. Between 1830 and 1834, during the reign of William IV, the very practical (but notoriously dull) architect Edward Blore was tasked with completing the work that John Nash had started. The degree to which Blore followed Nash's

Fig. 5
Three of the many dolls made by Baroness Louise Lehzen and Princess Victoria when she was a child. Some represent historical figures and friends; others are characters from the ballet

Fig. 6
The Archbishop of Canterbury and the Lord Chamberlain informing Princess Victoria of her accession

blueprint is unclear. However, he certainly applied some of his own designs and added a new storey above the main portico, necessitating the removal of Nash's unpopular small dome. By introducing new spaces to the building, Blore began the process of turning George IV's scheme into a more functional royal palace, with room for a royal consort, state guests and a larger household. William IV never liked Buckingham Palace, however, and when the Houses of Parliament burned down in 1834 he offered it to the government as a replacement. They declined. Like his brother, William IV did not live long enough to see Buckingham Palace fully completed, so when Victoria took up residence in 1837, the Palace had remained unoccupied for almost 20 years, despite nearly £600,000 having been spent on its remodelling.

Fig. 7
View of Buckingham Palace from St James's Park,
painted nine years after Victoria's accession

Fig. 8
View of Buckingham House in 1819, the year of Victoria's birth

Indeed, the Palace that Victoria inherited was not only unloved and unlived-in but partially unfinished. Large areas remained undecorated and many essential fixtures and fittings, such as sinks, fireplaces, carpets and curtains, were missing. Aware of the Palace's unfinished state, Victoria's ministers had urged her to consider remaining at Kensington Palace a little longer until Buckingham Palace could be brought up to a more suitable standard. However, Victoria, eager to begin her new life in her new Palace, remained resolved to move in immediately, remarking rather jovially when informed that there was almost no furniture that she would be happy to bring her own.

One item of furniture that Victoria did, however, commission was a throne for her Throne Room. In 1837 Parliament approved a payment of £1,187 to the London-based upholsterers Dowbiggin & Co. for a throne, platform and canopy. Surmounted by a

LEFT
Fig. 9
The new throne commissioned by
Queen Victoria for her Throne Room
at Buckingham Palace

ABOVE CENTRE
Fig. 10
Queen Victoria's Collar of the Order
of the Bath, designed to be worn just
below the shoulders, to match the
necklines of her formal dresses

ABOVE RIGHT
Fig. 11
Queen Victoria's Star
of the Order of the Bath

gilt-wood crown and the Queen's 'VR' cipher, the throne is intricately decorated with carved acanthus and oak leaves as well as the British emblems: the rose, the shamrock and the thistle (Fig. 9). At the same time, the Queen commissioned new insignia, including a Star and a Collar, for each of the five British Orders of Chivalry (Figs 10 and 11). Although insignia already existed, Victoria needed collars that reflected her diminuitive stature and could be worn with women's fashions of the day. Indeed, as well as being considerably lighter and with smaller links, Victoria's new collars were longer so that they could be worn just below the shoulders, to match the necklines of her formal dresses.

As well as the seemingly unending list of missing fixtures, fittings and furniture (running from chairs and tables to stoves, doors and chopping blocks), numerous practical and structural problems continued to be reported throughout 1837–8. It is important to remember that until this point George IV's version of Buckingham Palace had never been tested, so teething problems were inevitable. Among these, the distance between the kitchen and the dining room was found to make it impossible to serve the Queen a hot meal, most of the Palace's water closets did not work and most of the newly installed fires (the main source of heating in the Palace) could not be lit without the chimneys smoking. In addition to being empty and cold, the Palace smelled. The aroma of oil and glue from the storerooms and workshops on the north of the Palace permeated the Queen's private apartments (situated directly above). A more general fault in the ventilation system meant that air was drawn up from the drains when the fires were lit, creating a foul, sewer-like stench politely referred to in the reports as 'effluvia'. A letter from the Board of Green Cloth, which came under the management of the Lord Steward, neatly summarised the situation in 1837: 'The Building has been finished in a manner very destitute of those conveniences and prerequisites which Windsor Castle and the Pavilion possess, and which are considered indispensable in a Royal Palace.'

The serious physical problems with the Palace were only exacerbated by major issues in the organisation and running of the Royal Household. In 1841, Baron Stockmar (Fig. 12), one of the Queen's senior advisers, composed a lengthy

Fig. 12
Baron Stockmar, who first came to England in the service
of Victoria's uncle, Leopold, and became one of her closest advisers

memorandum describing the complete 'absence of system' which he had observed (Fig. 13). Instead of one person having overall charge of the Palace staff, responsibility was split between the Lord Chamberlain, the Lord Steward and the Master of the Horse. With so many chiefs, no one was quite sure who was responsible for which bits of the Palace and, based on archaic precedents, staff were apportioned in an irrational fashion. For example, while the cooks, kitchen clerks and porters were under the jurisdiction of the Lord Steward, by an anomaly the livery porters and under butlers (who worked closely with the kitchen staff) were accountable to the Master of the Horse. This system resulted in various oddities and inefficiencies. Broken windows stayed broken for weeks and there was often no one to attend to the comfort of the Queen's guests, who were left wandering around the Palace with nobody to show them to or from their rooms. In one case, Stockmar recalled that, 'having been sent one day by the present Majesty, to Sir Frederick Watson, then the Master of the Household, to complain – that the dining room was always cold – he was gravely answered, "You see properly speaking, it is not our fault, for the Ld steward lays the fire only, and the Ld Chamberlain lights it."' This culture seemed to extend across the Royal Household, with Stockmar describing the Palace staff as unregulated and at liberty to 'commit any excess or irregularity'.

In 1840, the problems at the Palace came to a head when a serious security breach was reported. Only weeks after the birth of Queen Victoria's first child, a small boy, subsequently identified as Edmund Jones, was discovered under

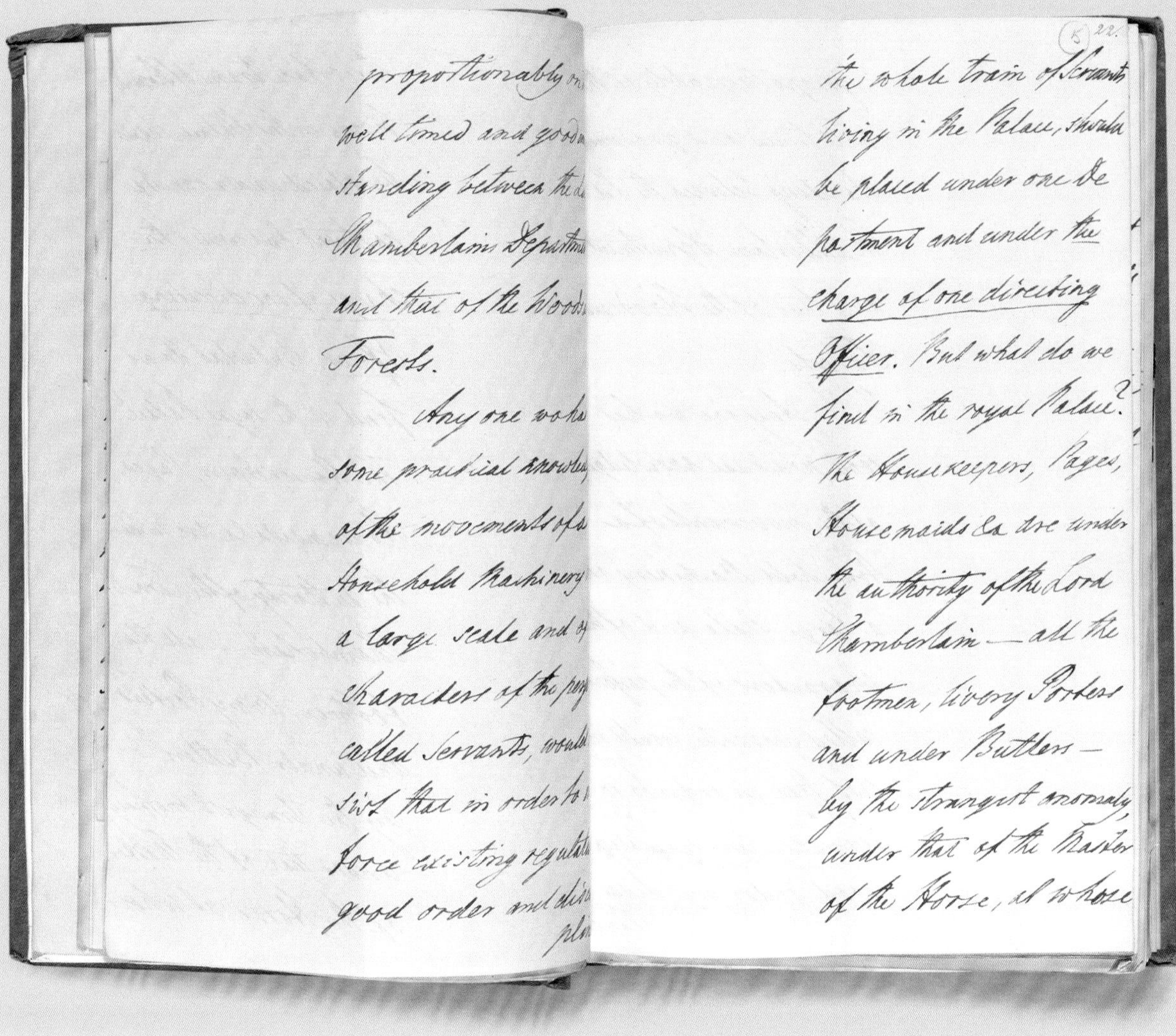

proportionably [...]
well turned and good [...]
standing between the [...]
Chamberlain Department
and that of the Woods [...]
Forests.

    Any one who has
some practical knowledge
of the movements of [...]
Household Machinery [...]
a large scale and of
characters of the per[...]
called Servants, would
see that in order to [...]
force existing regula[tions]
good order and dis[...]
    pla[...]

the whole train of Servants
living in the Palace, should
be placed under one De
partment and under the
charge of one directing
Officer. But what do we
find in the royal Palace?
The Housekeepers, Pages,
Housemaids &c are under
the authority of the Lord
Chamberlain — all the
footmen, livery Porters
and under Butlers —
by the strangest anomaly,
under that of the Master
of the Horse, il whose

Fig. 13
Memorandum written by Baron Stockmar
about the state of the Royal Household in 1841

a sofa in the Queen's private sitting room. He claimed he had climbed over the wall at Constitution Hill and entered the Palace through a broken window. He later boasted that he had not only eaten food from the Palace kitchens but had sat on the Queen's throne and 'heard the Princess Royal squall' in the Queen's private apartments.

Remarkably, given the evident chaos, Victoria seemed delighted with her new Palace. Indeed, in many ways it was an improvement on her rooms at Kensington, which were riddled with black beetles, referred to by Victoria as her 'Kensington friends'. Shortly after she moved in, Victoria recalled how much she liked Buckingham Palace's 'high, pleasant and cheerful' interiors and the large garden, with which her dog Dash was particularly taken (Fig. 14). Seemingly oblivious to the smells, and only occasionally complaining of the cold, Victoria delighted in even the smallest of decorative enhancements. 'It is all so changed', she wrote in 1840 on seeing her newly refurbished apartments, 'my rooms fresh painted and the doors altered ... and beautiful chintz curtains and furniture; it looks like a new house, and so pretty.' In fact, two years earlier Victoria had come to the defence of her new Palace in the face of a series of reports compiled by Sir James Clark (the Queen's Physician) regarding the substandard conditions he encountered. 'Clark', she wrote, 'told Lord M. [Melbourne] that people had complained of the heat at my Parties! Now this is a direct falsehood for B.P. is reckoned the coolest house in London, and everybody was surprised how cool it was. Talked of alterations to the garden, which I said I wouldn't hear of, etc., and other nonsense of Clark's.' In the end, it was not until Prince Albert's arrival in 1840 that any significant changes were made to either the infrastructure or the organisation of the household at Buckingham Palace. Like her Palace, Queen Victoria was not, either personally or in her mastery of the constitution, the finished article, something to which she privately admitted on the day of her accession:

ABOVE
Fig. 14
This painting of Dash, Victoria's pet dog, was given to her by her mother in 1836

Since it has pleased Providence to place me in this station, I shall do my utmost to fulfil my duty towards my country; I am very young and perhaps in many, though not in all things, inexperienced, but I am sure, that very few have more real good will and more real desire to do what is fit and right than I have.

Aware of her strength of character but also her lack of experience, Victoria sought essential advice from two men in particular: her uncle, King Leopold of the Belgians, and her Prime Minister, Lord Melbourne (Figs 15 and 16). Both men fulfilled a paternal role for the young Queen, who had grown up without a father, and Victoria evidently admired them greatly. 'How I wish I had time to take <u>minutes</u>', she lamented, 'of the very interesting and highly important conversations I have with my Uncle and with Lord Melbourne; the sound observations they make, and the impartial advice they give me would make a most interesting book.'

RIGHT
Fig. 15
Portrait miniature depicting
Leopold I, King of the Belgians,
uncle to both Queen Victoria
and Prince Albert

FAR RIGHT
Fig. 16
Portrait miniature depicting
Lord Melbourne, Prime Minister
at the time of Queen Victoria's
accession, who acted as mentor
to the Queen

Although Victoria and Leopold had corresponded for many years, when Victoria became Queen, Leopold's letters started to include practical advice on Sovereignty as well as more general niceties. With regard to conducting official business, 'The best plan', he wrote to his niece only days after her accession, 'is to devote certain hours to it ... I think you would do well to tell your Ministers that for the present you would be ready to receive those who should wish to see you, between the hours of eleven and half-past one.' Later on in the same letter he suggested that, wherever possible, important questions should never be answered in haste but should be ruminated on overnight. 'Good habits formed now', he concluded, 'may forever afterwards be kept up.' Leopold's business-like approach to Sovereignty is something Victoria continued to apply for the rest of her life.

While Leopold provided Victoria with more general advice on queenship, Lord Melbourne acted as her tutor in matters of politics. Gallant, handsome and charming, Victoria took an instant liking to her new Prime Minister, describing him in a letter to Leopold as 'not only a clever statesman and an honest man, but a good and kind-hearted man, whose aim is to do his duty for his country and not for a [political] party'. Over the next couple of years they formed a close friendship, with Melbourne dedicating many hours of the day to either writing to Victoria or mentoring her in person on the workings of the Cabinet, often over supper at Buckingham Palace or in her private apartments. In particular, he ensured that Victoria understood her position as a constitutional monarch and the fine line she must tread between advising and dictating to Parliament.

Victoria's determination to make Buckingham Palace not only her home but also her official headquarters made it only natural that, just a year after her succession, the coronation procession should, for the first time, leave for Westminster Abbey from the Palace itself. For the occasion, the carriage procession to the Abbey (a tradition introduced by William IV seven years earlier) was extended, starting at the gates of Buckingham Palace before proceeding up Constitution Hill, along Piccadilly and down Whitehall towards Westminster – the route used by all subsequent monarchs, and designed to make the Queen more visible to her people. Indeed, thousands of them

Fig. 17
View of Westminster Abbey from Buckingham Palace,
painted by Queen Victoria

lined the streets in specially built stands, with an estimated 400,000 spectators arriving in central London. To entertain them, a programme of free events was organised, including a balloon ascent and firework display in Green Park. For the first time, the coronation had become a truly national spectacle, designed as a day of mass celebration and attracting attention from beyond London. Moreover, it initiated the establishment of Buckingham Palace as a central image in the consciousness of the nation.

After a 90-minute carriage ride through the streets of London, the Queen, dressed in a white gown, red velvet mantle and diamond circlet, arrived at Westminster Abbey (Fig. 17). Preceded by Lord Melbourne, the Queen entered the Abbey, where she was officially received by the Archbishop of Canterbury (Figs 18 and 19). Victoria then retired to St Edward's Chapel, a dark space immediately behind the altar, where she changed out of her velvet kirtle and mantle and into her supertunica, a beautifully embroidered sleeved robe made from the finest cloth of gold (Fig. 20). Bare-headed, Victoria, now dressed in her ceremonial vestments, re-entered the Abbey to sit in the Coronation Chair (historically known as St Edward's Chair) where the dalmatica, a long golden cloak, was placed over her shoulders, and the orb, sceptre and ring were presented (Fig. 23).

LEFT
Fig. 18
Pencil drawing by Queen Victoria of her coronation procession in Westminster Abbey, showing the Queen in her red velvet and ermine mantle, preceded by Lord Melbourne

BELOW
Fig. 19
Panoramic view of Queen Victoria's coronation procession in Westminster Abbey

FAR LEFT
Fig. 20
The supertunica worn by Queen Victoria at her coronation. The full-length gown, worn over a plain white dress, was made from cloth of gold, trimmed with gold lace and metal spangles

OPPOSITE TOP
Fig. 21
This painting by George Hayter captures the moment immediately after the crowning of Queen Victoria in Westminster Abbey. The Queen is seated on the Coronation Chair, wearing the Imperial State Crown

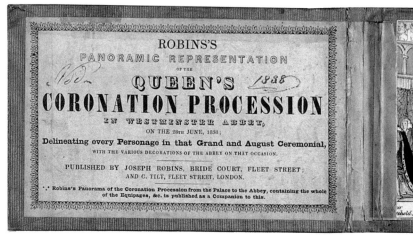

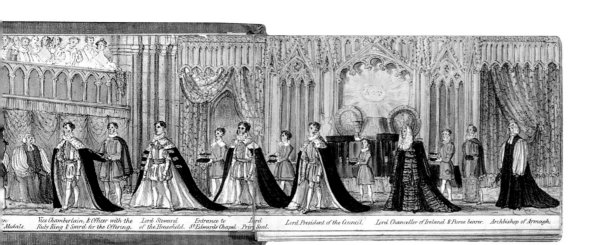

Vice Chamberlain, & Officer with the Ruby Ring & Sword for the Offering.   Lord Steward of the Household.   Entrance to St Edwards Chapel.   Lord Privy Seal.   Lord President of the Council.   Lord Chancellor of Ireland & Purse bearer.   Archbishop of Armagh.

Finally, a new State Crown, adapted from that worn by her uncle, William IV (Figs 22 and 24), was placed on her head at which point the peers and peeresses put on their coronets, 'a most beautiful and impressive moment', the Queen recounted, and one captured in a painting by George Hayter (Fig. 21).

Despite the young Queen's grace and composure, the coronation itself was shambolic. Victoria later complained that the Bishop of Durham, who was central to the ceremony, 'never could tell' the Queen 'what was to take place'. Indeed, not only was the Queen presented with the orb too soon but towards the end of the ceremony she had to be brought back from St Edward's Chapel as the Bishop of Bath and Wells had turned over two pages of the litany by mistake, thus missing out a large part of the proceedings. A general lack of professionalism amongst the Queen's ladies and ministers was also noted. Two of the Queen's train-bearers could be heard chatting throughout the service and Lord Lyndhurst, the former and future Lord Chancellor, forgot to back away from the Queen's presence and, as Benjamin Disraeli rather cattily reported, could be seen 'drinking champagne out of a pewter pot' after the ceremony, 'his coronet cocked aside, his robes disordered'. Perhaps the most painful mishap of the ceremony was committed by the Archbishop of Canterbury who, in an attempt to place the coronation ring on the Queen's third finger rather than her little finger, rammed it so hard that she winced with pain and had 'the greatest difficulty' removing it in the robing room afterwards.

Following the ceremony, the Queen, dressed in a purple velvet gown and carrying her orb and sceptre, returned to Buckingham

Fig. 22
Print of the Imperial State Crown
of Great Britain which was made for the
coronation of Queen Victoria in 1838

Palace amidst cheering crowds. She later recorded how the number of people on the street seemed to have increased: 'The enthusiasm, affection and loyalty', she noted that evening, 'was really touching.' Out of the public eye, the Queen went straight upstairs to give her dog, Dash, a bath, before returning to the state apartments for supper. The day, one she would always remember 'as the proudest of my life', finished on her mother's balcony (on the north of the Palace and offering one of the best views out towards Piccadilly) watching the fireworks light up the sky above Green Park. The first stage in Buckingham Palace's public makeover was complete – the once-ridiculed building project now resplendent as an important part of the monarch's coronation, as it has been ever since.

ABOVE
Fig. 23
Queen Victoria's coronation ring

RIGHT
Fig. 24
The frame of the Imperial State Crown made for Queen Victoria, which originally incorporated jewels from George I's State Crown of 1715

Building a
Family Home

The 1840s, opened by the most popular and public of royal events, the Queen's marriage, marked a distinct shift in the function and appearance of Buckingham Palace and, in time, its grounds.

Queen Victoria first met her future husband, Prince Albert, in May 1836 when he was presented, alongside his brother Ernest, at a ball given by the Duchess of Kent in honour of her daughter's seventeenth birthday. Victoria and Albert were first cousins (the Duchess of Kent was the sister of Albert's father), and King Leopold of the Belgians, who was uncle to them both, was particularly keen on the match. Following their first meeting Victoria showed only a passing interest in Albert, describing him as attractive, with 'a very sweet mouth', but rather portly in comparison to his brother and, on account of his retiring early from the dancing, sadly lacking in spirit and stamina. It was not until their second meeting three years later that the couple fell in love, Victoria heartily declaring when she saw Albert that he was 'excessively handsome' with beautiful eyes which set her heart 'quite going'. Only five days after this meeting Victoria and Albert were engaged and just over a month later Victoria formally announced to her Council her intention to marry. With Albert, Victoria had not only found love, but someone who would prove to be a devoted, like-minded and constant companion.

Following their engagement, Edward Blore quickly set to work making Buckingham Palace ready for Albert's arrival. Three hundred men were reportedly employed to convert the suite of rooms on the north side of the Palace into accommodation for the Queen and her future husband. The work involved displacing the Queen's mother: 'the rooms at Buckingham Palace where she lives', Victoria explains in her journal, 'must be Albert's'. A plan produced between 1843 and 1847 details the precise arrangement of the royal couple's private apartments which ran along the length of the north wing, with the Queen's rooms in the west and Albert's in the east. While both Victoria and Albert had their own private sitting and dressing rooms, the Queen's suite also contained areas for her Dresser (at this date, Marianne Skerrett) and her Ladies-in-Waiting as well as an audience room for conducting state business (Figs 25 and 26). At the other end of the corridor, Prince Albert's rooms, which took up less space, closely reflected his

Fig. 25
Queen Victoria's sitting room,
depicted in 1848

interest in the arts, containing both a cabinet for the display of art objects and a painting room.

With their rooms taking shape, on 10 February 1840 Victoria and Albert were married in the Chapel Royal at St James's Palace. Following the service, a wedding breakfast was held at Buckingham Palace. Perhaps the most notable part of the celebration was an enormous wedding cake, measuring almost 3 metres in circumference and weighing around 136 kilograms (Figs 27 and 28). The cake was topped with figures of Queen Victoria, Prince Albert and Britannia shown in the act of blessing the royal marriage. The couple spent their wedding night at Windsor Castle, the Queen recording in her journal that evening: 'My <u>dearest</u> <u>dearest</u> <u>dear</u> Albert ... He clasped me in his arms, and we kissed each other again and again! ... Oh! this was the happiest day of my life!'

At Buckingham Palace, Victoria and Albert went to great lengths to create a happy, domestic environment for their young family. Neither of them had experienced particularly happy upbringings – Albert's mother had left when he was only five – and, together, they were determined to give their children the childhood they had never had.

LEFT
Fig. 26
Prince Albert's dressing room,
pictured in around 1860

ABOVE
Fig. 27
One of the wedding cakes produced for
the marriage of Queen Victoria to Prince Albert

RIGHT
Fig. 28
Box containing a piece of
Queen Victoria's wedding cake

Within weeks of their marriage, Queen Victoria became pregnant and on 21 November 1840 Princess Victoria was born at Buckingham Palace. Victoria did not enjoy being pregnant. She loathed the physical discomfort, frequently referring to the 'sufferings and miseries and plagues' of childbearing. More than that, she hated being taken away from her official duties to spend long periods of time confined to her rooms at Buckingham Palace. During these confinements, all of which were overseen by the same nurse, Mrs Lilly (Fig. 29), Victoria was forced to delegate her duties to Albert, something that clearly pained and frustrated her. In a letter written to the Princess Royal in 1858, she describes pregnancy as akin to being 'pinned down', her 'wings clipped … only half oneself'. With a busy official programme, Victoria also frequently had to appear at important state events while heavily pregnant, something that would have been particularly wearing given her tiny, barely 5-foot frame. On 7 June 1844, only two months before the birth of her fourth child, Prince Alfred, the Queen entertained some 250 guests at a State Ball held at Buckingham Palace. Festivities continued into the early hours, and the Queen noted in her journal that evening that 'Naturally, I felt very tired'. Queen Victoria had nine children in 17 years, eight of whom were born at Buckingham Palace.

Victoria and Albert were loving and conscientious parents. Their devotion to their children reflected the prevailing wisdom of the time, namely that childhood was a distinct and important phase of life (an observation that originated in the eighteenth century) and that the family unit was integral to a happy and functional society. That Victoria and Albert so publicly embodied the values of the period made them immensely popular. Numerous prints emphasising the Queen's role as wife and mother and depicting the royal family as a picture of modern, domestic harmony were produced and circulated throughout the 1840s (Figs 30 and 31). The effect of the Queen's family on her widespread popularity was not lost on Victoria. In 1844 she commented, 'They say no Sovereign was more loved than I am

Fig. 29
Mrs Lilly, the nurse who attended all Queen Victoria's confinements, photographed in 1864

(I am bold enough to say), and that, from our happy domestic home – which gives such a good example.'

Unlike pregnancy, Victoria evidently enjoyed motherhood. 'Children,' she concluded, 'though often a source of anxiety and difficulty are a great blessing and cheer and brighten up life.' This sentiment is certainly reflected in the Queen's early journals and sketchbooks, which are full of heartfelt references to her children's wit, beauty and intelligence. Perhaps the greatest testament to

Fig. 30
Hand-coloured lithograph which, when illuminated, reveals Queen Victoria, holding an infant in her arms, attended by Prince Albert and a nurse

Victoria's maternal affection is a volume of 224 drawings of the royal children, all produced by the Queen and lovingly collated, annotated and bound into a single album. The drawings provide an intimate record of everyday activities in the royal nursery. Prince Arthur, whom the Queen privately admitted was her favourite child (describing him as the 'most precious object to me on earth'), is depicted with particular

Fig. 31
Hand-coloured lithograph with movable parts that reveal Victoria and Albert playing with three of their children. Such novelty prints were very popular in the early years of Victoria's reign

TOP
Fig. 32
Sketch by Queen Victoria of her
third son, Prince Arthur, dated 1851

ABOVE AND RIGHT
Fig. 33
The first shoes worn by Prince Albert Edward
(later King Edward VII), with an inscription
on one of the soles

delicacy, his increasing mobility celebrated in a series of quickly worked sketches (Fig. 32). The Queen also took a keen interest in her children's development, recording their achievements and milestones in her letters and journals as well as preserving childhood souvenirs. In 1842, Victoria noted that 'The Baby' (referring to Albert Edward, the future King Edward VII), 'now stands up at a sofa or chair & crawls extremely well & quickly'. A month earlier, the Queen had lovingly set aside a pair of his shoes, with the words 'The Prince of Wales's first Shoes worn July 1842' inscribed on one of the soles (Fig. 33). Some of Victoria's commissions were a little more unusual, the most pertinent of these being a set of marble hands and feet designed to capture the folds and curves of her children's limbs (Figs 34 and 35). The Queen was also fond of commissioning bespoke frames or boxes to hold her children's treasures. Around 1860, a highly intricate gilt-metal casket was produced at Victoria's request to house the royal children's first teeth. Within the main box, five of the satin-lined compartments have been dedicated to Queen Victoria's children, each containing a series of teeth wrapped in paper (Fig. 36).

Like Victoria, Albert was a notably doting and affectionate parent. While Albert the man was serious and studious, Albert the father was surprisingly comical and extroverted. At Buckingham Palace he could often be seen pushing one of his children around the nursery in a basket or running about in the garden playing hide-and-seek or sporting a butterfly net. Albert also enjoyed taking the older children on outings, not just educational excursions but recreational jaunts to London Zoo and Madame Tussaud's. Victoria was clearly taken aback and delighted by how naturally Albert had taken to fatherhood, commenting in a letter to her uncle Leopold in 1841, 'I think you would be amused to see Albert dancing [Vicky] in his arms ... he makes a capital nurse (which I do not, and she is much too heavy for me to carry), and she always seems so happy

TOP
Fig. 34
Marble sculpture of Prince Alfred's
left arm, made in 1845

ABOVE
Fig. 35
Marble sculpture of Victoria, Princess Royal's left foot,
made in 1843

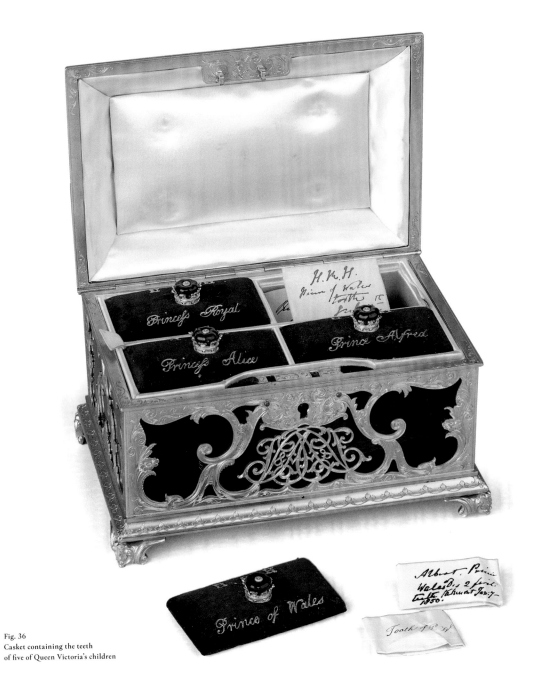

Fig. 36
Casket containing the teeth
of five of Queen Victoria's children

Fig. 37
Engraving after Edwin Landseer's pastel drawing of Prince Albert and the infant Victoria, Princess Royal

to go with him.' The Princess Royal proved to be a particular favourite of Albert's: he would visit her, sometimes twice daily, in the nursery and, in the evenings, put her on his knee at the piano so that she could 'touch the Keys … which delighted her'. A pastel produced by the eminent painter Edwin Landseer at a similar date to this anecdote beautifully captures the intimacy between father and daughter (Fig. 37).

Fig. 38
Cradle commissioned by Queen Victoria for her fourth
daughter, Princess Louise, who was born in 1848. The
elaborate carving along the sides of the cradle includes
emblems of the royal houses of Britain and Saxe-Coburg
and symbols associated with sleep

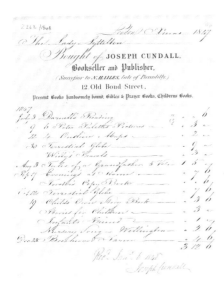

Fig. 39
Invoice listing toys and books purchased for the royal nursery in 1847

While Victoria and Albert's vision of an ideal family home manifested itself most fully at Osborne House on the Isle of Wight – purchased by the royal couple in 1845 as a domestic seaside retreat – Buckingham Palace, like all the Queen's residences, was enthusiastically adapted to accommodate the needs of the children and treated as much as a family home as it was the Queen's head office. One important addition to the Palace was the royal nursery. For the birth of the Princess Royal, the Queen's Dressing Room was temporarily fitted out as a nursery until more suitable rooms could be made ready. Later, as more children arrived, a series of rooms on the north side of the Palace, originally intended for servants, was transformed for this purpose, though the makeshift result was rather cramped. Plans of the Palace reveal that by 1847 the nursery consisted of 12 rooms: a number of bedrooms and recreational areas as well as a kitchen, dining room and bathroom. It is hard, today, to appreciate that, during this period, the nurseries of the upper classes were not just single rooms but entirely separate households, with younger children sleeping and eating all their meals within the nursery itself. At Buckingham Palace, the royal children had a remarkably lenient upbringing in comparison to other households of the time, seeing their parents several times a day rather than existing almost entirely independently from them.

Like most new parents, Victoria and Albert seem to have enjoyed decorating and furnishing the new nursery. As well as a number of cradles, mostly commissioned or purchased on the birth of each new child, the nursery was also equipped with highchairs and feeding equipment in addition to grooming products such as soaps, combs and brushes. While some of the items purchased for the nursery were essentially domestic, others clearly reflected the status of their royal owners.

The cradle commissioned by the Queen on the birth of Princess Louise in 1848 is one of the finest examples of its kind, painstakingly carved with emblems from the royal houses of Britain and Saxe-Coburg, all interspersed with motifs associated with sleep (Fig. 38). A number of surviving invoices, now housed in the Royal Archives, provide further evidence of the sorts of toys, books and games that were purchased for the nursery under the watchful eye of the nursery superintendent. An example from 1847 includes a farm made from beechwood (delivered just in time for Christmas) as well as various books and two terrestrial globes (Fig. 39).

From 1843 the nursery was run by Lady Lyttelton, formerly Lady Sarah Spencer, who was already employed as a Lady of the Bedchamber to Queen Victoria. 'Laddle', as she was affectionately known to her royal charges, replaced the former superintendent Mrs Southey, who had failed to maintain order in the nursery and whom Albert had accused of negligence in relation to the health of the Princess Royal. Recently widowed, and with five children of her own, Lyttelton was already well versed in looking after children and, much to the Queen's relief, fitted seamlessly into the royal family, quickly restoring order to the nursery. Amongst other things, she introduced a system of reporting on the day's activities (much like a nursery school would today), composing a memorandum each evening that the Queen would then read the following morning. The nursery was also staffed by a large number of nursemaids, all of whom reported to Lyttelton and many of whom appear in Queen Victoria's sketchbooks (Fig. 40). A photograph taken outside Buckingham Palace in 1848 shows the royal children with one of their nurses, Mary Ann Thurston (Fig. 41). Appointed in 1845, Mrs Thurston was much liked by Victoria and remained with the family for many years. She was photographed again ten years later, holding an infant Princess Beatrice (Fig. 42).

Fig. 40
Watercolour of Princess Beatrice, Victoria's youngest child, in the arms of her nurse, painted by the Queen in 1858

By 1845, only five years into their marriage, Victoria and Albert already had four children and it was becoming increasingly clear that Buckingham Palace was no longer large enough to accommodate their rapidly expanding family. In pursuit of her desire for a suitable family home, amongst other reasons which will be discussed later, the Queen was about to initiate a further alteration in the shape of the Palace, one that would make a lasting impression on the national perception of the royal family.

On 10 February, Victoria and Albert wrote a letter to the Prime Minister, Sir Robert Peel (a draft of which survives in the Royal Archives), concerning 'the urgent necessity of doing something to Buckingham Palace'. In this letter the Queen highlighted:

Fig. 41
Group portrait of Victoria and Albert's first six children outside Buckingham Palace with their nurse, Mary Ann Thurston, photographed in 1848

Fig. 42
Princess Beatrice photographed with Mary Ann Thurston in 1858

the total want of accommodation for our growing little family, which is fast growing up. A large addition such as alone could meet the case could hardly be occupied before the Spring of 1848, if put in hand forthwith, when the Prince of Wales would be nearly seven, the Princess Royal nearly eight years old, and they cannot possibly be kept in the nursery any longer. A provision for this purpose ought, therefore, to be made this year

On receipt of this letter, Sir Robert (Fig. 43), doubtful that the Queen's request would meet with either public or Parliamentary approval, urged Victoria to wait until the following year when Parliament might be more likely to vote in her favour. 1845 was proving to be particularly tumultuous. Peel had recently reintroduced Income Tax and was about to repeal the Corn Laws, a decision that would lead to his resignation as Prime Minister in 1846. Added to this, the general public were still reeling from the extravagance of Victoria's uncle, George IV, while early reports of a potato famine in Ireland had begun to reach the government offices. Undeterred, the Queen carried on against the advice of her Prime Minister and asked Edward Blore to compile a report on the Palace, accompanied by a series of practical recommendations. As Peel had predicted, Blore's observations, concluding that the Palace was too 'cramped', were derided by the media. An article in the *London Daily News* compared the Queen's predicament to the 'Old Woman' who 'lived in a shoe and had so many children she didn't know what to do', and, in response to Blore's observation that the poor royal children were living in an attic, mischievously reported that they must, forthwith, be 'rescued from the indignity' and 'allowed to grow without fear of becoming, like the reel in the bottle, too big to be got out'.

Fig. 43
Noted for his reforms in the sphere of law and order, and for the establishment of the London Metropolitan Police Force when Home Secretary, Sir Robert Peel served two terms as Prime Minister between 1834 and 1846. At first finding him 'rather pompous' and slow, Queen Victoria gradually began to appreciate his statesmanship

Fig. 44
The Royal Pavilion at Brighton was built by George IV as a seaside retreat.
It was sold to the town of Brighton in 1850

Despite Peel's objections, and the faint public animosity towards Victoria's proposals, on 13 August 1846 Parliament granted Victoria an initial payment of £20,000 towards completing and extending Buckingham Palace on the condition that Brighton Pavilion should be sold to offset some of the costs (Fig. 44). By 1847 plans were already afoot to sell the building and its grounds and in 1850 the Pavilion was finally sold to the town of Brighton for £53,000. As a further means of economising, it was suggested that the contents of the Pavilion, including all its fixtures as well as the furniture, should be integrated into the new extension to the Palace. As a result, the rooms on the front of the Palace still have a distinctly Eastern feel that is incongruous with the rest of the building.

In 1846, Edward Blore, having concluded that it would not be possible to extend the existing footprint of the Palace, submitted plans for an entirely new building linking the ends of the existing wings and thus creating a fourth side to Buckingham Palace. His plans were approved and work began soon after. The rooms were to be a mixture of private and public spaces, with state guest rooms taking up much of the principal floor with private spaces above. The main corridor, running the length of the building and latterly renamed the 'Princesses' Corridor', would provide, as the Queen had requested, rooms for her older daughters once they had outgrown the nursery. A photograph taken in 1873 shows one such room, which is known to have been occupied by Princess Beatrice (Fig. 45).

Work on the new wing progressed slowly. In January 1849 the Queen reported that the passage leading from the new staircase in the north-east corner of the Palace had been completed and by June a number of paintings had been hung in the new apartments. Blore's plans for this new east wing also necessitated the removal of Nash's Triumphal Arch, designed for George IV as a flamboyant entrance to the Palace. For many months it remained in fragments in store, before eventually being re-erected in 1851 at the entrance to Hyde Park where it remains today and is now known as the Marble Arch.

One of the first rooms to be completed in Blore's new wing was the Pavilion Breakfast Room. On 10 June 1849 the Queen took breakfast in her new room, describing it as 'very handsomely fitted up with furniture &c. from the Pavilion at Brighton, including the Chinese pictures, which were on the Dining room walls there, the doors with the serpents &c. which had belonged to that room. A dragon has been painted on the ceiling to harmonise with the rest'. A watercolour by James Roberts, produced in 1850, provides a record of the room's early appearance (Fig. 46). Despite the ornate decoration, the room's domestic function is suggested by the toy horse in the foreground and the highchair just visible in the far left-hand corner. It was to this family breakfast

Fig. 45
A bedroom used by Princess Beatrice
at Buckingham Palace, photographed
in 1873

Fig. 46
The Pavilion Breakfast Room in 1850

room, situated directly below the newly configured nursery, that the royal children would be brought on birthdays and special occasions. On 1 May 1852, Prince Arthur's second birthday, the Queen recorded in her journal how 'Dear Mama … came to breakfast & little Arthur came in, in a white frock, looking very dear. His birthday table was covered with toys & we gave him a little Grenadier's Bear Skin'. A portrait by Winterhalter, painted the following year, shows the young prince in a similar child-sized bearskin and Guards' uniform (Fig. 47). Prince Arthur would go on to have a career in the military and allegedly never missed a guard change, which the royal children could watch from the nursery window.

Fig. 47
Prince Arthur depicted in uniform in 1853, wearing a bearskin similar to the one given to him on his second birthday by his parents, Queen Victoria and Prince Albert

Fig. 48
The completed East Front of
Buckingham Palace, photographed
by the renowned Crimean War
photographer, Roger Fenton,
in around 1858

Fig. 49
Queen Victoria's birthday table at
Buckingham Palace in May 1846

By 1850 the majority of the work on the new East Front had been completed (Fig. 48). As well as providing space for the Queen's family, it marked an important step in the Palace's transformation from private residence to public monument. On 1 May 1851, the day of the opening of the Great Exhibition, the Queen and Prince Albert appeared on their new balcony (an addition to Blore's plans suggested by Albert), to crowds of onlookers, for the very first time, starting a tradition that continues to this day. In enclosing and concealing the U-shaped Palace, so closely linked with the extravagant spending of her uncle, George IV, Queen Victoria had effectively given the Palace a makeover. Blore's new wing became the public face of the Palace, a façade that would soon become synonymous with Queen Victoria and a symbolic focal point for the nation.

As well as being fitted out with a nursery, Buckingham Palace played host to a number of family events. In April 1846 Princess Alice's third birthday was marked with a party at Buckingham Palace, complete with a conjuring performance and 'little gifts' for the guests. A month later Victoria celebrated her twenty-seventh birthday with an elaborate present table laid out in 'the little room, next to Vicky's schoolroom'. Besides gifts from Albert and the Duchess of Kent, the Princess Royal presented her mother with a handwritten letter while Albert Edward read her a story. The table is recorded in a watercolour by Joseph Nash (Fig. 49).

Perhaps the most lavish children's birthday party to be hosted at Buckingham Palace was the Fancy Ball of 1859, held in honour of Prince Leopold's sixth birthday. The children who attended came in a variety of costumes: Prince Leopold and Prince Arthur were dressed as the two sons of Henry IV while Princess Helena and Princess Louise wore Swiss costume (Figs 50 and 51). The Queen evidently took a particular interest in what everyone was wearing, describing the assembly as, on the whole, 'becomingly dressed' but rather mischievously noting that the 'Bernstorff boy' had been costumed 'awfully ... in a petticoat of white satin ... a wreath of roses & "fowl's wings" ... carrying a bow & arrow, to represent Cupid!'. The event is immortalised in a watercolour by Eugenio Agneni, the poor little 'Bernstorff boy' probably identifiable as the figure with a headdress and wings in the centre-left of the composition (Fig. 52).

LEFT
Figs 50 and 51
Hand-coloured photographs showing
Prince Arthur, Prince Leopold, Princess
Louise and Princess Helena dressed in
their costumes for the Children's Fancy
Ball held to celebrate Prince Leopold's
sixth birthday in 1859

BELOW
Fig. 52
The Children's Fancy Ball.
Princess Louise, Princess Helena,
Prince Arthur and Prince Leopold
can be seen to the bottom left and
right of the painting

Fig. 53
Albert's library in the late 1860s

Fig. 54
Albert's organ room in 1873. The organ, made by Gray & Davison in 1841,
can be seen at the far end of the room

Victoria and Albert also adapted the rooms at Buckingham Palace to accommodate their varying interests and leisure activities. Both had their own libraries (Fig. 53), while Albert also had his own private organ room (Fig. 54). Made by Gray & Davison in 1841, the organ was designed in two parts to fit around the fireplace.

One of the features of the Palace that the entire family enjoyed was the expansive garden (Fig. 55). While the Queen delighted in activities such as walking and dining, as well as drawing and painting in the garden (Fig. 56), Prince Albert had a penchant for more active outdoor pursuits, such as ice-skating on the lake in the winter and playing skittles with the children in the summer. On occasion, Albert went to more extreme lengths to stay fit. In June 1842, the Queen recorded in her journal that just before

Fig. 55
Victoria and Albert with eight of their children, photographed by Roger Fenton in
the gardens of Buckingham Palace in May 1854. From left to right: Prince Leopold,
Prince Alfred, Princess Helena, Princess Alice, Prince Albert Edward, Prince Arthur,
Princess Louise, Queen Victoria, Victoria, Princess Royal and Prince Albert

Fig. 56
Watercolour by Queen Victoria of
a flower bed viewed from a window
at Buckingham Palace, 1853

leaving Windsor for London, 'Albert went early with our Cousins, to bathe & swim in the Thames', something 'he had done for several days'.

The Queen's children made similar use of the Palace grounds (Figs 57–59). Attached to the Royal Mews, the garden was particularly well situated for them to enjoy equestrian activities. A child-sized, donkey-drawn barouche, presented to the royal children by Queen Adelaide, Victoria's aunt and the widow of William IV, is known to have been used across the royal residences, while a photograph taken by the Florentine photographer Leonida Caldesi shows a two-year-old Princess Beatrice enjoying her first pony ride outside one of the conservatories. The garden was also the perfect place for informal gatherings and parties. A photograph taken in 1854 shows the Prince of Wales and Prince Alfred in the garden with a group of friends.

The garden also presented the royal couple with a more novel location for artistic experimentation. In 1842 Victoria and Albert commissioned a small cottage in the

Fig. 57
Princess Beatrice, photographed on her second birthday, shown taking her first pony ride

Fig. 58
Prince Albert Edward (the future King Edward VII) and Prince Alfred with friends in the gardens of Buckingham Palace in the summer of 1854

grounds of the Palace, designed to be an oasis from the hustle and bustle of London life. By the end of 1842 their plans had changed and Prince Albert, in his capacity as the Chairman of the the Fine Arts Commission, suggested that the cottage might instead be used by a select number of artists as a laboratory for fresco painting. The contract for decorating the new Palace of Westminster was offered as the ultimate prize. In 1843 eight British artists were asked to decorate parts of the cottage, now renamed the pavilion, and from 1844 Ludwig Grüner, Prince Albert's art adviser, took over the task of co-ordinating their efforts as well as preparing additional designs. The pavilion was destroyed in 1928 and is now only known to us through a series of coloured prints (Figs 60–62). Nevertheless, it remains a fascinating illustration of Victoria and Albert's colourful and ambitious use of the Palace and its grounds and of their support for the furthering of the Fine Arts.

Fig. 59
A donkey barouche, given to the children of Queen Victoria by
her aunt, Queen Adelaide, the widow of William IV

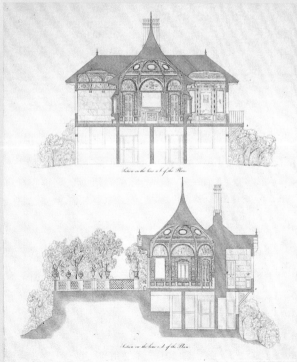

TOP
Fig. 60
View of the garden pavilion in the grounds of Buckingham Palace in 1847

LEFT AND OPPOSITE
Figs 61 and 62
Prince Albert commissioned artists to decorate the rooms inside the pavilion using the Italian technique of fresco. The central octagon (opposite) was decorated with scenes from John Milton's masque, *Comus*

Entertaining at
Buckingham Palace

Royal hospitality has always fulfilled a special role in public life, particularly at Buckingham Palace. The redesigned building (Fig. 63) did far more than provide a suitable home for the young Queen's growing family. It also enabled Victoria to turn her plan for a modern monarchy into reality. At Buckingham Palace she demonstrated a different kind of Sovereign power, one that relied on mutual relationships and shared values rather than on displays of wealth and military might. It was royal statecraft reimagined for the industrial age. In this new vision for the monarchy, a ball or dinner at the Palace was never just a social occasion; it was an opportunity for the arts to flourish, the wheels of diplomacy to turn, or for a charitable cause to benefit – sometimes all at the same time. The magnificent entertainments that characterised the first part of Victoria's reign transformed Buckingham Palace into the most glittering court in Europe (Fig. 64).

ABOVE
Fig. 63
The East Front of Buckingham Palace in 1852, after the completion of Blore's design and the removal of Nash's Triumphal Arch to its present position at the edge of Hyde Park as the Marble Arch

RIGHT
Fig. 64
Guests arriving at the State Ball held on 5 July 1848 ascending the Grand Staircase to the State Rooms on the first floor

An accomplished singer and pianist, music had always been one of Victoria's great loves (Fig. 67). Her arrival at Buckingham Palace meant that she was now free to indulge the passion on her own terms – with one small issue. It had been 20 years since the State Rooms were last used for entertaining and their neglect showed. Undaunted, Victoria held her first musical evening at Buckingham Palace on 15 July 1837, only two days after moving in, with a performance by Swiss pianist Sigismond Thalberg, who was on a concert tour of Europe at the time. He had recently won a mock musical duel against Franz Liszt in Paris, sealing his reputation as one of the foremost musicians of his day.

Thalberg joined the royal party after dinner and Victoria was supremely moved by his performance. 'Never, never did I hear anything at all like him!', she recorded in her journal: 'I sat quite near the piano and it is quite extraordinary to watch his hands, which are large, but fine and graceful. He draws tones and sounds from the piano which no one else can do. He is unique.' She found him 'extremely gentlemanlike' and 'very agreeable to talk to'.

A few days later, Victoria hosted her first proper concert. She invited her favourite opera singers, including Luigi Lablache, who had given her singing lessons at Kensington Palace, to sing from a selection of Italian operas (Fig. 65). The performance took place in the central room of the State Apartments, overlooking the Palace gardens. It was 'the middle room, which has a sort of dome', recorded Victoria. She was pleased to discover that the acoustics were ideal for music, and in time all concerts, except the very largest, were held here so that it eventually became known as the Music Room. Encouraged by the success of her musical evenings, the young Queen decided to make them a weekly occurrence. She also revived the tradition of the royal private band to entertain at formal and informal gatherings (Fig. 66). But even when there were no professional musicians present, the more talented among Victoria's inner circle could be relied on to perform. She expected her Maids of Honour to be able

ABOVE
Fig. 65
Queen Victoria commissioned this portrait of Luigi Lablache, one of the most celebrated singers of his generation, in 1852. Lablache gave regular singing lessons to Victoria from 1836 to 1857, when he began to suffer from ill health

Fig. 66
A music stand made for Victoria's private band

to sing and sight-read at the piano on command, a rather daunting prospect for all but the most accomplished and confident player.

When it was time to hold her first ball, on 10 May 1838, Victoria found herself feeling rather nervous. While waiting for the doors to open to announce her entrance, she was suddenly seized by the thought of what awaited her on the other side. 'I felt a little shy in going in,' she wrote, 'but soon got over it, and went and talked to the people'. Once again, she had secured the services of the most sought-after musician in London. Johann Strauss (the elder), the father of the Viennese Waltz, performed with his band in what is now the Blue Drawing Room. Social protocol barred the unmarried Victoria from actually dancing any of the waltzes, but she loved listening to the music. Fortunately, there were no barriers to her taking part in the quadrilles in the Picture Gallery. She stayed until 4am, displaying a stamina on the dance floor that stayed with her even in old age.

Fig. 67
This grand piano by S. & P. Erard was intended as a showpiece to form part of the furnishings of the State Rooms. Both Queen Victoria and Prince Albert were accomplished pianists

Fig. 68
Victoria was a great admirer of opera
and opera singers, and, from an early
age, sketched artists she had seen in
performance. Here she depicts the
Swedish soprano Jenny Lind in the
role of Maria in Donizetti's *La Fille
du Régiment*

Two more balls followed in quick succession, one to celebrate
Victoria's birthday and the other her coronation. Both evenings featured
Strauss and his daring waltzes, signalling to all present that the young
Queen wasn't afraid to embrace modern ideas. At the last ball Strauss
ended with a specially composed waltz that opened to the tune of 'Rule,
Britannia!' and finished with 'God Save the Queen'. Victoria danced until
dawn (albeit only the quadrilles), enjoying herself enormously in the
process. In only a year she had breathed fresh life into the Palace, giving
it new purpose and filling its rooms with music and laughter. The matter
of the antiquated kitchens and the practicalities of feeding large groups
of people had yet to be properly addressed, but she was ready to begin
entertaining on the scale expected of a queen.

The day after their engagement, Queen Victoria and Prince Albert
could be found at the piano, taking turns at singing and playing. Albert
thrilled his fiancée by presenting her with a song he had composed
himself. The happy couple were the perfect foil for one another. Not
only were Victoria and Albert interested in similar cultural pursuits, they
were both doers rather than mere talkers. 'I love to be employed; I hate to be idle', the
Queen once admitted in her journal. Rather than being content to reflect fashionable
opinion, Victoria and Albert set their own agenda for what they wished to promote.
Throughout their 21-year marriage Buckingham Palace was the backdrop for
their shared love of the arts. Music was a particular beneficiary, since a
performance at the Palace all but guaranteed widespread fame for a young
performer or new work.

Queen Victoria's enchanting sketches of her favourites, such
as the Swedish opera singer Jenny Lind (Fig. 68), are a testament to
the lasting friendships with composers and musical performers that often
began with an invitation to perform at the Palace. None of them, however,
could replicate the close relationship that developed between Victoria and
Albert and the German composer Felix Mendelssohn (Figs 69 and 70).

Fig. 69
Felix Mendelssohn, one of many famous musicians
and composers who performed for the royal couple
at Buckingham Palace in the 1840s and 1850s

Fig. 70
In this engraving, Prince Albert is portrayed playing the organ for Queen Victoria
and Felix Mendelssohn at Buckingham Palace

They met for the first time on 16 June 1842, by which time Mendelssohn (who, like Mozart, had been a child prodigy) had already become a firm favourite with British audiences. He had recently performed his so-called 'Scottish' symphony (*Symphony No. 3 in A minor*), inspired by a visit to the ruins of Holyrood Abbey in Edinburgh, when the invitation came from Buckingham Palace. Victoria had been longing meet him and Mendelssohn's first impression didn't disappoint. He was delicate-looking, 'with a fine intellectual forehead,' she wrote, and 'very pleasing and modest'. When he sat down to play, Mendelssohn put on a virtuoso performance that stunned his listeners. 'He asked us to give him a theme, upon which he could improvise', recorded Victoria. They mischievously suggested 'Rule, Britannia!' and the Austrian national anthem. He began without the slightest hesitation, producing one variation after another, each one more elaborate than the last, until: 'At one moment he played the Austrian Anthem with the right hand [while] he played "Rule, Britannia!", as the bass, with his left!'.

The other notable event to take place at Buckingham Palace in 1842 was the Plantagenet Ball, the first of three magnificent costume balls held by Victoria and Albert. Fancy-dress parties and masquerades were then all the rage in Europe. The country was also suffering an economic downturn, and Victoria was looking for a way to help London's independent craftsmen and artisans, especially those in the clothing trade.

Victoria and Albert decided to give their ball a historical theme. Their ultimate choice of characters revealed the careful thought that had gone into the selection. They appeared as the fourteenth-century Queen Philippa and Edward III, the royal couple most closely associated with England's golden age of chivalry, due at least in part to Edward founding the Order of the Garter in 1348. It was an inspired choice for setting the tone of the new reign. In their private lives, Philippa and Edward were famously devoted to one another and their 14 children. As rulers, they had formed one of the most successful partnerships of the Middle Ages, with Philippa governing as Regent during Edward's military campaigns abroad.

Victoria's dress for the occasion was designed by the foremost expert on historical costume, James Robinson Planché, and inspired by examples found in medieval illuminated manuscripts. Such was the surrounding excitement that, rather than keeping the gown a secret, she agreed to let it be exhibited publically in Hanover Square two days before the actual ball. The rush to see the dress brought Mayfair to a standstill, with long lines of carriages clogging the streets around the square.

Planché's insistence on complete accuracy led to some unintentional hilarity. One 'knight' ordered his suit of mail from a theatrical props and costumes company and ended up with a flimsy ensemble covered in silver spangles. Another arrived at the ball so weighed down by his steel amour that he could hardly move. Victoria herself struggled in her medieval heels and only managed to survive through one quadrille. But the overall effect of the costumes was considered an unqualified success (Fig. 71). 'Nothing could have gone better', she wrote in her

Fig. 71
Tabard embroidered with the royal arms of England worn by a Page at the Plantagenet Ball and subsequently by Albert Edward, Prince of Wales, when a child

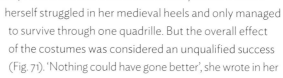

RIGHT
Fig. 72
Queen Victoria and Prince Albert dressed as Edward III and his consort, Queen Philippa, for the Plantagenet Ball held on 12 May 1842

journal, notwithstanding the heels, 'It was a truly splendid spectacle.' To commemorate the ball, Victoria commissioned Edwin Landseer to paint a portrait of the couple in their costumes standing in front of the thrones (Fig. 72). A slow painter at the best of times, Landseer was still working on the portrait in 1845 when Victoria and Albert held their second ball to benefit the London clothing trade, known as the Powder Ball on account of its eighteenth-century dress theme (Figs 73–76).

The magnificent pageantry of the Powder Ball couldn't hide the fact that, for all its gilded splendour, Buckingham Palace lacked the grand entertaining rooms of the Tuileries Palace in Paris or the Hofburg in Vienna. Victoria's patience finally snapped after one of her favourite dances ended up being ruined by the great crush of people. 'We then danced,' she recorded in her journal, 'or rather more tried to dance "Sir Roger de Coverley" in the Gallery, but it was much too crowded and great confusion ensued, so that we were obliged to give it up.' The embarrassing incident supported her complaint to Sir Robert Peel in 1845 that ignoring the building's many shortcomings was no longer acceptable. As well as more space for Victoria and Albert's growing family, and other improvements besides, the Palace needed 'a room, capable of containing a larger number of those persons whom the Queen has to invite in the course of the season to balls, concerts, etc.' What she couldn't say was that the kitchens were unable to keep up, and the heat produced at the balls and concerts was almost intolerable. It wasn't only the neck collars and petticoats that wilted; foreign visitors were appalled by the crude conditions that guests were expected to endure. Modernising the Palace had become a matter of national pride.

These improvements required a large and complicated building project, and Victoria's hope of the work being finished by 1848 was wildly optimistic. Construction of the new ballroom hadn't even begun when the Queen and Prince Albert held their final costume ball, the Stuart Ball, on 13 June 1851 (Figs 77–80). Though still a success, the physical toll of a Buckingham Palace ball was beginning to make people think carefully about accepting another invitation. The lessening of the crowds had one beneficial result, however: there was more room to dance and the beautiful costumes could be seen more easily. The historical period chosen for this occasion was the late seventeenth century.

Figs 73–75
Victoria and Albert dressed in the fashions of 1745 for the
second costume ball that they held at Buckingham Palace,
known as the Powder Ball. The Queen is shown with her hair
powdered and is wearing the ribbon and Star of the Garter

Fig. 76
In this watercolour of the Powder Ball, held at Buckingham
Palace on 6 June 1845, Victoria and Albert are lined up
in the Throne Room with their guests, the duc and duchesse
de Nemours, to dance the royal minuet, the second dance
of the evening

Figs 77 and 78
For the Stuart Ball, held in 1851, Victoria asked Eugène
Lami to design costumes for herself and Albert. The
Queen's silk and lace gown, decorated with gold braid,
silver fringing and seed pearls, was inspired by the court
of Charles II

Fig. 79
This sketch, made by Victoria in her journal, depicts herself
and Albert (to the left and centre of the drawing) in their
costumes for the Stuart Ball. The third figure (to the right
of the drawing, labelled 'Charles') may be her half-brother,
Prince Charles of Leiningen

Fig. 80
The Stuart Ball took as its theme the court in the reign of Charles II. As well
as designing Victoria's dress, Eugène Lami was closely involved in the planning
of the ball, and his watercolour here shows eight couples, all in identical dress,
approaching the Queen and Prince Albert, who are standing on a dais to the
right of the painting

Once again, the emphasis was on British manufacture and materials. The Restoration era, so-called because it marked the return of the Stuart kings to the throne following the end of the Commonwealth that had resulted from the English Civil War, had been a great moment for British lace-making. Victoria and Albert hoped that the ball would provide a much-needed boost to the lace industry in Devon, centred on Honiton. Albert's entire costume was British-made, and the only notable exception to Victoria's was the pink, silver and gold brocade on her petticoats, which was woven in India.

Although the ballroom was still a few years away, by the end of 1851 the other longed-for additions and refurbishments were complete. The renovated Palace offered visiting heads of state a far more welcoming and comfortable experience than in previous years. Fortunately, during Emperor Nicholas I's visit to London in June 1844, the Russian Emperor had spent the majority of his time at Windsor Castle (Figs 81–84). 'He had really only come to visit me,' Victoria wrote afterwards, 'and it could not but be a good thing.' The visit had taught her a valuable lesson about the importance of personal relationships in the high stakes arena of international diplomacy:

> By seeing one another, one gets to know people's characters, their faults and their good qualities; one gets to understand their feelings and consequently what are their own actions, and what are not.

Emperor Nicholas returned to St Petersburg believing that he had persuaded the Queen and her government to take Russia's side in any European quarrel. By 1853, the Crimean War had begun, pitting Russia against Turkey, with France threatening to join the Turks.

Fig. 81
Prince Albert leaving Windsor Castle
on his way to review the household
troops in the Home Park, accompanied
by Emperor Nicholas I, during the
Emperor's visit to Britain in 1844

Fig. 82
The 1844 room at Buckingham Palace,
named to commemorate Emperor
Nicholas's visit

Even though the Queen and Prince Albert were not in favour of war – the country had been at peace since 1815 – they also recognised that if the country remained neutral it could leave British interests and allies dangerously exposed. 'The year opens gloomily as regards the affairs of Europe', Victoria wrote in her journal on New Year's Day 1854, 'War seems almost inevitable.'

Just as the Queen had feared, Britain joined the fight in early 1854 – but not on the side of Russia, which the government and public regarded as the aggressor. On 28 February, Victoria and Albert, accompanied by four of their children, stood on the balcony of Buckingham Palace to salute the troops before they departed for the Crimea (Fig. 85).

The Crimean War was the first conflict to be fought using the advances of the industrial age: with mass-produced weapons, long-range cannons, iron ships, steam trains and rapid communication provided by the telegraph. But at home, Queen Victoria faced the same dilemma confronted by her sixteenth-century ancestor, Elizabeth I, during the Anglo-Spanish War. As a ruling queen, Victoria was expected to lead her subjects but as a woman she was required to display the proper behaviour demanded of her sex. She had to create a wartime role for herself that met both needs.

Victoria chose to make a virtue of her femininity and set an example for the nation with her personal and public efforts to alleviate the suffering of the troops. She knitted woollens for the soldiers, sent provisions to the Crimean army camps, inspected military hospitals,

LEFT
Fig. 83
Following his visit, Nicholas I sent a mosaic table and this large porcelain vase as gifts to Queen Victoria and Prince Albert. Decorated with matt and burnished gold, the vase is painted with views of the imperial palaces of Peterhof and Tsarskoe Selo

ABOVE
Fig. 84
Medal commemorating the Emperor's visit

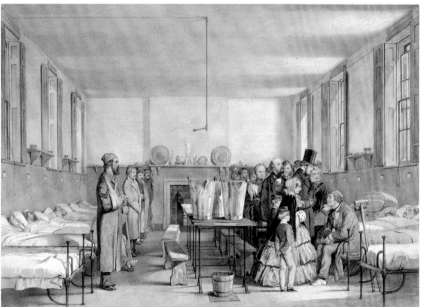

TOP
Fig. 85
The Scots Fusilier Guards on the
forecourt of Buckingham Palace,
bidding farewell to Queen Victoria
and Prince Albert in 1854

BELOW
Fig. 86
Victoria and Albert visiting Fort Pitt
Military Hospital in Chatham, Kent,
in March 1855, where they met
wounded soldiers who had returned
from the Crimea

wrote letters of condolence to the bereaved, and donated money to charitable organisations (Fig. 86). Victoria greatly admired the nurses who went out to the Crimea on their own initiative, women such as Florence Nightingale and Mary Seacole. In 1855 she sent Miss Nightingale a gold enamelled brooch, which bore the motto 'Blessed Are the Merciful', to stand in place of a war medal.

By 1855, however, the war was not going well. Britain and France were unlikely military allies, having spent the best part of the previous two centuries at war with one another. The government did not always see eye to eye with Emperor Napoleon III, particularly his desire to take command of the armies in the Crimea himself. No amount of delicate diplomacy could change the Emperor's mind. The only solution was to invite him to make a State Visit to Britain where frank discussions could take place amidst the opulent surroundings of the new Buckingham Palace.

With so much riding on the State Visit, Victoria and Albert were determined to ensure that both the Palace and Windsor Castle were shown to their greatest advantage (Figs 87–89). On 15 April, the day before the arrival of Napoleon and his wife, the Empress Eugénie, at Windsor, Victoria made a thorough inspection of their apartments, commenting: 'A good deal of new furniture has had to be got, though there was much fine old furniture in store, which has [been] carefully renovated'. Still, even with all the preparations that had been made, her old anxieties returned as she waited on the steps of the Castle to greet the French entourage. It was a relief when she saw Eugénie emerge from the carriage 'evidently very nervous'. To Victoria's surprise, she found the visitors easy to talk to: 'We got on extremely well at dinner, & my agitation soon easily went off.'

A genuine friendship had developed by the time the visit moved to Buckingham Palace on 19 April. The days seemed to pass by very quickly. Victoria found the shy Eugénie 'graceful' and 'unaffected'; 'she always puts herself in the background'.

Figs 87–89
Great preparations were made to
welcome the French Emperor,
Napoleon III, and his wife, the
Empress Eugénie, to Buckingham Palace
on the occasion of their State Visit
to England in 1855

OPPOSITE AND ABOVE
The Tapestry Drawing Room and
bedroom prepared for the Empress

BELOW
The bedroom prepared for
the Emperor

Napoleon III fascinated her: 'he is a very extraordinary man ... I might almost say a mysterious man ... possessed of indomitable courage, unflinching firmness of purpose, self-reliance, perseverance, and great secrecy'. For his last night in Britain the Queen and Prince Albert held a concert in the Music Room and a buffet supper for 600 people.

Napoleon had come to Britain with the aim of flattering Victoria into agreeing to whatever he proposed. As it happened, during the course of his stay it was the Emperor who was persuaded to drop his Crimean plan. Four months later the Queen and Prince Albert paid a reciprocal visit to Paris, the first for a British monarch since 1431 (Figs 90 and 91). The icy relationship between the two countries had finally thawed.

The Crimean War ended in January 1856 with victory for the allies (Fig. 92). The previous year, Victoria had invited a group of wounded soldiers to Buckingham Palace: 'Albert walked round with me, as well as Col: Wood, & I spoke to each man, questioning them as to their wounds' (Fig. 93). Their courage and suffering had affected her badly:

Figs 90 and 91
Queen Victoria, Prince Albert and their two eldest children visited Paris in August 1855 as the guests of Napoleon III. The watercolour shows the Queen and her family entering Paris under a triumphal arch. The Queen made the sketch of the Emperor during the visit

OPPOSITE TOP
Fig. 92
On 9 July 1856 the three battalions of Guards who had returned from the Crimea marched from Pall Mall to Buckingham Palace, where the royal family had gathered on the balcony

OPPOSITE BOTTOM
Fig. 93
Queen Victoria and Prince Albert, with their three eldest sons, inspecting wounded Grenadier Guards who had returned from the Crimean War, in the Marble Hall, Buckingham Palace, in February 1855

ABOVE LEFT
Fig. 94
This military jacket was worn by
Queen Victoria when reviewing the
troops on their return from the Crimea,
and is thought to have been designed
by Prince Albert

ABOVE RIGHT
Fig. 95
The Crimean Medal was conferred on
all officers and men who had served
in the war. Each medal bore the clasps
of those actions in which the recipient
had been involved. In this example, all
five clasps are shown: Alma, Balaklava,
Inkerman, Sebastopol and Azoff

LEFT
Fig. 96
Watercolour showing Queen Victoria
presenting the Crimean Medal on Horse
Guards Parade, 18 May 1855. The
Queen wished to present the medal to
many of the men herself, and on this
occasion she distributed 768 medals

'I had meant to make some kind of general speech, but I was so agitated, that it all stuck in my throat'. In a show of appreciation, Victoria commissioned a military-style dress of scarlet and gold which she wore at military reviews (Fig. 94). She also oversaw the creation of two new awards, the Crimean Medal for all members of the armed forces who served in the war (Figs 95 and 96), and the Victoria Cross which remains Britain's highest military decoration for valour (Figs 97 and 98).

In 1856 the new Ballroom and Ball Supper Room were finally ready (Figs 99–101). The design of the new annexe had been awarded to the architect James Pennethorne, who had previously worked on the Palace during George IV's reign under the pupillage of John Nash. His addition fitted seamlessly with the old apartments, creating the impression that the new rooms had always been there. Encouraged by Albert, who regarded the project as his 'Creation and Child', Pennethorne laboured to combine the Prince's love of history and tradition with his insistence on contemporary standards of comfort. The Ballroom, 33.5 metres long and 18 metres wide, was the largest room in the Palace and could easily accommodate the fashion for wide crinoline petticoats,

ABOVE
Fig. 97
This was probably the prototype for the Victoria Cross, submitted to the Queen in February 1856 for her comments

LEFT
Fig. 98
The first ceremony to distribute the Victoria Cross, which recognises outstanding valour throughout all ranks of the armed forces, took place in Hyde Park in June 1857. Queen Victoria can be seen here on horseback, as she presents the medal to a Captain of the Mast in the Royal Navy

allowing women to dance or sit on banquettes without ruining their dresses. The proportions of the room were classical in design, the layout medieval in effect with its two-storey-high ceiling and thrones at the far end facing the music gallery, and the decorations inspired by the Italian Renaissance. But the acoustics, lighting and ventilation were the very latest in modern technology.

The beautiful red silk hangings, decorated with the national flowers, on the walls were the result of a collaboration between Prince Albert and his German art adviser, Ludwig Grüner. The two men were also responsible for commissioning the Raphael-inspired cartoons that were mounted between the high-level windows, and for the decorations on the ceiling. Grüner personally oversaw the work to manufacture the Ballroom's ten magnificent gilded candelabra (Fig. 102). When lit, they burned a total of 430 wax candles, a feat that was only possible with Pennethorne's new air circulation system. The Ball Supper Room was even more exuberant in its decoration.

Figs 99–101
Sir James Pennethorne prepared a series
of designs for the Ballroom and Ball
Supper Room in 1852, which were
signed off by Prince Albert

Perspective view of the interior of the Ballroom

Design for the organ at the east end of the Ballroom

Perspective view of the exterior of the Ballroom
and Ball Supper Room

Fig. 102
The second ball held in the new Ballroom at Buckingham
Palace, 17 June 1856. The interior decoration was inspired
by Italian Renaissance design. Victoria can be seen seated
on the dais at the far end of the Ballroom

ABOVE

ABOVE
Fig. 103
Print of the exterior of the new Ballroom, 1856,
showing the South Front, railings and pillars

LEFT
Fig. 104
The Ballroom as designed by Sir James Pennethorne
and decorated under Prince Albert's direction,
photographed in 1873. The room was later completely
redecorated on the instruction of King Edward VII

In contrast to the brilliant red of the Ballroom, a softer tone predominated, accentuated by the marbled walls of pink and green. The *pièce de résistance* was the shallow domed ceiling, which was painted with gold stars and exotic birds against a rich blue background.

In 1856 Queen Victoria and Prince Albert decided to celebrate the return of peace with a series of balls in the new Ballroom. The second ball was held on 17 June 1856. Queen Victoria wore an elegant but simple gown for the occasion, made of white Indian muslin embroidered with gold flowers. Her headdress consisted of diamonds entwined with red and green leaves, complementing the joyful but restrained tone of her dress. The 2,000-strong guest list was vastly expanded from previous balls and included many members of the armed services and luminaries who had contributed to the success of the war. The ball began at 9.50pm, with the royal band playing 'God Save the Queen' as Victoria entered the Ballroom. Throughout the evening she made a point of speaking to those who had been wounded in the Crimea, such as 'a Captain Brown', she wrote in her diary, 'whose arm was shot off'.

The Ballroom exceeded Victoria's hopes. 'The ventilation is very good,' she wrote, 'and everybody could rest & could see' (Figs 103 and 104). Pennethorne's new kitchens were also a great success. Relieved of the daily struggle to meet demand, the Palace's 45 chefs had the room and facilities to demonstrate the true breadth of their culinary skills (Figs 105–108). The menu for the evening included a wide variety of dishes, from ox tongue to lobster salad, as well as jellies and aspics that had been moulded into fanciful shapes. The overall effect was

ABOVE
Fig. 105
Iced pudding à la Victoria, created by Charles Elmé Francatelli, Queen Victoria's confectioner, was an iced dessert, flavoured primarily with almonds and apricots and frozen in a melon-shaped mould before decoration with nuts and small fancy fruit-shaped ices

Fig. 106
The Alhambra table fountain, commissioned jointly by Queen Victoria and Prince Albert in the early 1850s. The horses were modelled on three of Queen Victoria's Arabs, which had been sent to her as gifts in the 1840s. The exotic plants were based on botanical specimens in Kew Gardens. The fountain is known to have been used at a dinner to celebrate Queen Victoria's Golden Jubilee in 1887

such that, 'Albert, even,' recorded Queen Victoria, 'who generally dislikes State Balls, enjoyed it, and I could have stayed up till 4, I am sure.'

The Crimean Balls marked the completion of Queen Victoria's Buckingham Palace. In making a home for her family that also served the aspirations of the nation, Victoria had ended up creating a new relationship between the Sovereign and the people. Ten years in the making, the renovations and additions had resulted in an architecturally splendid building that fully served the private, public, and state functions of the monarchy. The last word belongs to Benjamin Disraeli, who attended both the Crimean Ball of June 1856 and the first concert held in the Ballroom two weeks later. The usually cynical politician was in awe of what the Queen and Prince Albert had achieved, writing, 'It seemed to me that I had never seen before in England anything which realised my idea of a splendid court.'

ABOVE
Fig. 107
A dessert plate made by Minton, with Queen Victoria's
VR cipher in the centre of the design

RIGHT
Fig. 108
A selection of copper moulds similar to those commissioned
by Queen Victoria for the new kitchens

Resurgence

Ten months after the Crimean Ball, on 14 April 1857, Queen Victoria gave birth to Beatrice, her ninth and last child (Figs 109 and 110). As always, Prince Albert was her greatest source of support: 'My beloved one's love and devotion, & the way he helped in so many little ways, was unbounded,' she wrote. He alone knew the physical toll that Victoria's almost back-to-back pregnancies had exacted on her health. He was also the chief witness (and occasional victim) of their emotional cost as she struggled to balance her public and private roles. Victoria freely acknowledged her dependence on him. In 1858, she confessed to Vicky, her eldest daughter, that 'Papa has been and is everything to me'.

Prince Albert's love for Victoria was equally profound. But there was one great difference between them. Whereas the Queen was not afraid to assert herself and was once described as having 'veins of iron', Albert was quiet and melancholic despite his enormous appetite for hard work. In 1861 he was 42 years old, barely middle-aged, and yet he felt and often acted like a much older man. 'I do not cling to life; you do', he told Victoria when she tried to rouse him from his torpor. 'I am sure that if I had a severe illness I should give up at once; I should not struggle for life.' The Queen didn't – couldn't – bring herself to take his words seriously. The warning signs were there, however. The Prince had not been well all year and as the cold weather settled in for the winter he grew steadily weaker.

Albert probably contracted his final illness (believed at the time to be typhoid) at some point in November. Queen Victoria had battled the same disease when she was

Fig. 109
Watercolour by Queen Victoria of her youngest child, Princess Beatrice, in 1859

Fig. 110
Gold and enamel bracelet given by Prince Albert to Queen Victoria on her twenty-sixth birthday, 24 May 1845. The original miniature of their eldest child, Victoria, Princess Royal, was joined by portraits of their other children as they reached the age of four. Each miniature is inscribed with the name of the child and inset with a lock of hair

a 16-year-old girl. She clung to that fact as the team of doctors attending Albert became increasingly despondent about his survival. Albert breathed his last shortly before 11pm on Saturday, 14 December 1861, with his wife and children at his bedside. By midnight the great bell of St Paul's Cathedral was tolling the death knell for a senior member of the royal family (Figs 111–113). The City's churches answered back, and soon the same dull peel was echoing up and down the country. While Victoria and the family remained at Windsor, large crowds gathered outside Buckingham Palace, waiting patiently to sign the book of condolence. It was generally assumed that the funeral would take place in London, but the effort was beyond Victoria's strength. The mere thought of going to the Palace without Albert filled her with horror. She fled to Osborne, their beloved retreat on the Isle of Wight, for a few months and then to Balmoral in Scotland. She was paralysed by Albert's death, as though the only part of herself that mattered had died with him. 'How am I,' she wrote in desperation to her eldest daughter, 'who leant on him for all and everything – without whom I did nothing ... to live?' Her loneliness was worse than anything she had ever felt in childhood. The only way she could explain it to her daughter was to say: 'there is no one to call me Victoria now'.

The widowed Queen leant on her older children for support. But they were ill-equipped to cope with her grief. Victoria lamented to her friend, Queen Augusta of Prussia: 'my nature

Fig. 111
Sheet of mourning paper bearing the monogram
of Queen Victoria

LEFT
Fig. 112
Mourning ring in gold and black enamel containing
a portrait of Prince Albert, made for Queen Victoria
shortly after his death

RIGHT
Fig. 113
This marble portrait bust of Prince Albert by William Theed,
one of the royal couple's favourite artists, was commissioned
by Queen Victoria a fortnight after his death

ABOVE
Fig. 114
Queen Victoria and her close family
gathered around a bust of Prince Albert
following the wedding of the Prince
of Wales and Princess Alexandra

TOP LEFT
Fig. 115
Queen Victoria with her daughter,
Princess Louise, photographed at
Windsor Castle in March 1862.
The Queen is looking at a picture
of Prince Albert, who had died
three months earlier

LEFT
Fig. 116
Queen Victoria photographed
in the 1860s, wearing a black
mourning dress and veil

OPPOSITE LEFT
Fig. 117
The 1855 Room at Buckingham Palace,
A portrait of Emperor Napoleon III
can be seen on the wall to the right
of this photograph

OPPOSITE RIGHT
Fig. 118
Prince Albert's dressing room,
photographed in around 1864

is too passionate, my emotions are too fervent, and I feel in sore need of someone to cling to securely, someone who would comfort and pacify me'. Victoria's refusal to wear anything other than the deepest black reflected the depth of her despair (Figs 114–116). The Prince's rooms and belongings were kept exactly as he had left them. Each morning his watch was wound up, ink pen filled, and his hat, handkerchief and gloves laid out in readiness. In the evenings, the routine went in reverse, with staff putting out his shaving bowl and night clothes.

It was a year before the Queen felt strong enough to return to Buckingham Palace. Her daughter Princess Alice arranged it, 'thinking it would be best for me to have been once again in the house'. The visit, which was conducted with the greatest secrecy so that no one would know that the Queen was in London, produced mixed results. Victoria stayed only long enough to look over her old apartments. She was relieved to see that the two State Rooms commissioned by Prince Albert to commemorate the visits of Emperors Nicholas I and Napoleon III looked exactly as he had commanded (Fig. 117). 'My Darling's wise planning & arrangement of the 44 & 55 rooms, especially the latter, his favourite ... would last for futurity,' she wrote (as indeed they have). But the rest of the Palace felt alien to her. Her private apartments were 'All dismantled,' she wrote in bewilderment, 'and yet <u>all</u> the same' (Fig. 118).

Buckingham Palace may have looked the same from the outside but it had become a
ghostly shell on the inside. Up until the end of 1861 it had served as the epicentre of
the British monarchy, where the highest echelons and the greatest talents of society
met and socialised. Alas, no longer.

No functions were held at the Palace throughout 1862. Victoria relied on her
cousin, the Duke of Cambridge, to represent the Sovereign when a public occasion
absolutely required her presence. This is not to say that the Queen did no work
at all. Behind the scenes she remained a diligent monarch, reading her papers and
maintaining – sometimes to the chagrin of her ministers – her own strong opinions
about national and international affairs. Once, Victoria sharply reminded her Foreign
Secretary, Lord Russell, to 'take care that the rule should not be departed from, viz that
no drafts should be sent without the Queen's having first seen them'. But her dislike
of public appearances had turned into a full-blown phobia. At Osborne, she listened
to meetings of her Privy Council from an adjacent room, sending in messages instead
of speaking directly. Even talking became a burden to her. Entire mealtimes sometimes
took place in silence save for the odd cough or clink of metal on china.

The marriage of the Prince of Wales and Princess Alexandra of Denmark on
10 March 1863 proved to be exceptionally difficult for Victoria. She loathed the idea of
a London wedding and insisted on holding it at Windsor (Fig. 119). The Prince was only
allowed to invite a handful of guests, the rest being family or members of the household.
The moment the ceremony was over she disappeared, preferring to eat her lunch alone
with six-year-old Princess Beatrice.

Fortunately for Victoria, the Prince and Princess of Wales could assume most
of her public engagements. The first Drawing Room (a formal function at which ladies
were presented at court for the first time) in two years took place at Buckingham Palace
on 13 May 1863. The backlog of court presentations meant that poor Princess Alexandra
had to curtsey 600 times as an unending stream of debutantes in the full court dress of
white feathers, white silk dress and train, performed a complicated ballet of kissing and
deep curtseying at the same time.

Fig. 119
The wedding of Albert Edward, Prince of Wales, and Princess
Alexandra of Denmark at St George's Chapel, Windsor Castle,
10 March 1863. This was the first royal wedding to be held
in the Chapel. Queen Victoria, in mourning dress, watched
the service from the royal closet above the altar, seen in the
top centre of the painting

Fig. 120
Queen Victoria commissioned this portrait of herself and John Brown at Osborne House in the late 1860s
to illustrate the contrast between the happy times she had enjoyed there with Prince Albert and the grief she had
suffered since his death

Music returned in a very limited way to the Palace in 1864, with the Prince and
Princess of Wales dutifully hosting the state concerts instead of Victoria. But these
small concessions only highlighted the loss to public life caused by the Queen's unofficial
retirement. Victoria refused to open the Ballroom to celebrate Princess Louise's coming
of age. Nor did she let the King and Queen of Denmark stay at the Palace during their
visit to Britain. The King of Sweden ended up sleeping at the Swedish legation, and Prince
Humbert of Italy was forced to lodge in a hotel at Windsor.

The public began to protest. In March 1864 a prankster fixed 'for sale' placards to the
Palace railings, which read: 'These commanding premises to be let or sold, in consequence
of the late occupants declining business'. *The Times* felt obliged to concur with its general

sentiments, declaring that it was time for Victoria to attend to the needs of her subjects: 'For the sake of the Crown as well as of the public.' Privately, Prince Albert's former Lord-in-Waiting, Lord Torrington, told the editor of *The Times* that 'Everyone [in the Royal Household] appears more or less afraid to speak or advise the Queen'.

Although Victoria frequently insisted that she was 'utterly incapable' of doing anything more, the entry of John Brown, her Scottish personal attendant, into her life in 1865 helped to assuage her crushing loneliness (Fig. 120). For all his faults, Brown's bracing honesty and lack of obsequiousness made Victoria feel safe and secure. 'I don't like or want flattery,' she once wrote; what she needed (and missed) was a genuine connection.

The Queen's steady reliance on Brown made her life – and those of her courtiers – more bearable but it didn't lessen her desire to live in self-imposed retirement. She spent precisely two nights at Buckingham Palace between 1866 and 1867, both occasions after the State Opening of Parliament – an act that she performed under heavy protest. But in 1868 there was a glimmer of hope that her continued mourning might be coming to an end. The first sign was Victoria's favourable response to her flamboyant new Prime Minister, Benjamin Disraeli (Fig. 121). Victoria had thought him thoroughly 'obnoxious' in 1844. Two years later, she described him as that 'dreadful Disraeli' who was quite 'reckless and not respectable'. However, Disraeli, or Dizzy (as Victoria called him), valued female opinion, and in fact counted several women among his closest friends. He was also very good at reading emotions, a trait that served him well during his first Prime Ministerial meeting with Victoria in February 1868. Sensing the deep well of feelings behind Victoria's dignified mask, Disraeli played up to the drama of the moment by falling on his knees as he kissed her hand and declaring his eternal 'loyalty and faith'.

Disraeli made her feel as though theirs was a unique partnership that operated on a personal as well as a political

Fig. 121
Although Victoria did not warm to him at first, Benjamin Disraeli became one of her most trusted Prime Ministers

Fig. 122
This engraving shows Queen Victoria
meeting guests at a Drawing Room
at Buckingham Palace in March 1874

level. Almost in spite of herself, Victoria started looking forward to his visits. He was, she confided to her eldest daughter Vicky, 'full of poetry, romance and chivalry'. The Disraeli-inspired spring in Victoria's step manifested itself in a new willingness to spend more time fulfilling her public role at Buckingham Palace. The problem was how to take advantage of her change in attitude. A ball was out of the question; she couldn't bear to attend any of the concerts there, and she regarded the Drawing Rooms as a special instrument of torture (Fig. 122). After her second Drawing Room of the season on 1 April 1868 she wrote: 'There were 107 presentations & more than twice as many people besides. I had to leave before the end, feeling so utterly exhausted, & Alix [the Princess of Wales] took my place.'

If the interior of the Palace was still effectively closed off, that left only the garden for hosting large public events. Less exclusive than a Drawing Room and more informal than a ball or concert, a garden party allowed royal hospitality to be extended to many more people (Fig. 123). The Queen agreed to hold a garden party on 22 June 1868, but anxiety set in as the actual day approached: 'At 5 the alarming moment arrived & I went down into the Garden,' she wrote. 'The afternoon [was] splendid, & not too hot.' But now came the moment of truth. There were 'Quantities of people on the lawn whom I

had to recognise as I went along ... & after nearly 8 years seclusion, it was very puzzling & bewildering.' She listened to the Queen's Band, drank tea in one of the tents and, 'This over, I slowly walked back to the Palace, talking to people on the way'. Looking back, she felt as though the day had been 'a dream'. Perhaps so to her, but to Londoners it had been very real, and according to the *Illustrated London News*, which published two engravings of the day, an unmitigated success.

Fig. 123
A garden party was held to celebrate Queen Victoria's Diamond Jubilee
on 28 June 1897. The Queen and Princess Alexandra, the Princess of Wales,
can be seen in an open carriage to the right of this painting

Borne out of necessity and sorrow, the Buckingham Palace garden party would become one of the most popular summer events in the royal calendar. But for the Queen the initial charm lasted only as long as Disraeli was in power. His Tory government collapsed in November 1868, and with it much of Victoria's renewed zest for public life. The garden party experiment was repeated the following year, and was even more crowded than the first. Victoria, however, was feeling depressed again. 'Had to dress for the Garden Party, for which I felt quite unfit,' she wrote on 28 June 1869. 'I could hardly take anything & felt very wretched, & was in great pain the whole time.' Her complaints about being in pain were frequently dismissed by her family as being either made up or highly exaggerated. Yet after her death it was discovered that Victoria had suffered for decades from an untreated ventral hernia and prolapsed uterus – both almost certainly caused by her many pregnancies.

Victoria wrote in her journal on 24 May 1871, her fifty-second birthday, 'Alone, alone, as it will ever be!'. The Queen deeply resented the man who replaced Disraeli as Prime Minister. William Gladstone (Fig. 124) tried hard to build a relationship with Victoria but he undermined his efforts by what she called his 'overbearing obstinacy and imperiousness'. Victoria generally took against any of Gladstone's suggestions, especially when they pertained to Buckingham Palace or her public role as Sovereign. He repeatedly warned her that the 'stability of the throne', not to mention the 'social well-being of the country', depended on her carrying out the 'social and visible functions of the monarchy'.

Gladstone was right to be concerned. 1871 would prove to be one of the most difficult years of Victoria's reign. The calamities began with the abrupt exile of her fellow monarchs Emperor Napoleon III and the Empress Eugénie to Britain following France's defeat in the Franco-Prussian War. In April, the Princess of Wales

Fig. 124
William Ewart Gladstone held the office of Prime Minister four times between 1868 and 1894

gave birth to a boy who lived for one day. Instead of meeting with universal sympathy, Victoria was shocked to read about herself and her family in the most unflattering terms. There were calls in the national press for the monarchy to justify its existence. The country had become fed up with supporting a large, empty palace and an absent Queen. An anonymous pamphlet entitled 'What Does She Do With It?', which accused Victoria of shirking her public duties while hoarding money from the Civil List, captured the new mood of the country. The title became a popular slogan that was scrawled on walls and hoardings, particularly in the poorer parts of London.

The Queen's children (Fig. 125) decided to take matters into their own hands. During a family gathering at Balmoral in July they composed a letter, signed by all, to 'entreat you to enquire into the state of public feeling, which appears to us so very alarming'. They were just about to give it to Victoria when she fell seriously ill with a cascade of ailments, from an abscess on her arm to a throat infection. The incident frightened them and the letter was never delivered.

The Prince of Wales resolved the situation in the most unlikely manner. In late November he developed typhoid, and by an uncanny coincidence the illness reached its crisis point on 14 December 1871, the tenth anniversary of Prince Albert's death. The entire nation was gripped by the terrible drama that unfolded day by day and then hour

Fig. 125
The nine children of Victoria and Albert photographed with the Princess of Wales at the Rosenau, Coburg, in 1865. From left to right: the Princess of Wales, Prince Leopold, Princess Louise, Princess Beatrice, Princess Alice, the Prince of Wales, Prince Arthur, Victoria, Princess Royal, Prince Alfred and Princess Helena

by hour as he hovered between life and death. His recovery produced an outburst of rejoicing that temporarily made the country forget its exasperation with Victoria.

Prime Minister Gladstone persuaded Victoria to lead a national thanksgiving service at St Paul's Cathedral on 27 February 1872 (Figs 126 and 127). As usual, she balked at the idea of being on show and flatly refused to wear formal robes or ride in the state coach. But, as with the introduction of the garden parties, the day prompted stirrings of her old life. Her former confidence and delight in being able to use the Palace to share important moments with her subjects returned in force. Writing in her journal, she marvelled at 'the millions out, — the beautiful decorations, — the wonderful enthusiasm & astounding affectionate loyalty shown'. Massive crowds and cheering had accompanied the royal procession to and from Buckingham Palace. It was almost 4pm when the Prince and Princess of Wales said their goodbyes and left to go home to Marlborough House. The crowds outside the Palace hadn't lessened. Victoria made a decision. 'I went upstairs', she wrote, '& stepped out on the Balcony with Beatrice & my 3 sons, being loudly cheered.' The Queen had returned, but would she stay?

Victoria was delighted when Gladstone resigned in 1874 and Benjamin Disraeli became Prime Minister once more. If he was her Dizzy, she was his 'Faery Queen'. He was able to cajole Victoria into making more public appearances, and perhaps into enjoying them, too. The Queen agreed to open Parliament without the usual complaints. Her devotion to Albert's memory continued (Fig. 128), but the walls of grief were coming down.

LEFT
Fig. 126
The royal procession on its way to the service of thanksgiving held at St Paul's Cathedral to celebrate the recovery of the Prince of Wales from typhoid in 1872

ABOVE
Fig. 127
Finishing touches being put to decorations in Holborn in anticipation of the passing of the royal procession on its return to Buckingham Palace from St Paul's Cathedral

Though Victoria would not admit it to herself, she seems to have enjoyed being the focus of adoration. In 1876 the Queen and Disraeli agreed that for the prestige of the monarchy, particularly with regard to the imperial courts of Europe, and the stability of British rule in India, she should add 'Empress of India' to her titles (Fig. 129). Disraeli oversaw the passage of the Royal Titles Bill through Parliament; in gratitude Victoria made him the Earl of Beaconsfield. With the new title came new traditions and opportunities to reinvigorate Buckingham Palace. Over the next decade electricity was introduced, as well as a telegraph office and even a telephone. In 1878 Queen Victoria instituted the Imperial Order of the Crown of India, a medal awarded to women for service to India (Fig. 130). The first investiture took place on 7 May at the Palace. The 14 recipients 'came in, as they were named', recorded Victoria, and knelt down: 'I took the order from the cushion, & Lenchen & Beatrice, who were with me, helped to fasten them on, after which they kissed hands'.

Disraeli's death in 1881 left an emptiness in Victoria's life that none of her subsequent Prime Ministers came close to filling. But this time the loss did not send her back into her protective shell. She not only remembered the lessons learned during his premiership but improved upon them. Victoria reminded her ministers that her reign would reach its half-century in 1887. The last monarch to celebrate a Golden Jubilee had been George III in 1809. What better way to unite the country and raise public morale than to hold a national party?

The Queen offered to pay for the Jubilee herself – a wise move in light of the recent controversies over her absence from public life. Having charge of the purse-strings also gave her an extraordinary amount of control. Together with Prince Albert, Queen Victoria had transformed the monarchy from a remote and hidebound institution into an active defender of family, faith and patriotism. She insisted to her ministers that the celebrations should recognise the achievements of her 50-year reign as the matriarch of the nation-family (Fig. 131).

LEFT
Fig. 128
Gold, silver and enamel model of the Albert Memorial, Kensington Gardens, London. The monument was commissioned by Queen Victoria in memory of her husband, Prince Albert, and was opened by the Queen in 1872

ABOVE
Fig. 129
This official portrait of Queen Victoria as Empress of India was taken in 1876

RIGHT
Fig. 130
The Order of the Crown of India, established in 1878

BORN MAY 24,] HER MAJESTY THE QUEEN [CELEBRATION
1819—BEGAN TO REIGN   1837 — JUBILEE —1887 OF LONGEST REIGN, 1897

A. BASSANO   [COPYRIGHT]   OLD BOND ST. W

ABOVE
Fig. 134
Queen Victoria processing through Trafalgar Square from
Buckingham Palace, on her way to the Golden Jubilee service
held in Westminster Abbey on 21 June 1887 to celebrate
50 years of her reign

OPPOSITE
Fig. 135
Queen Victoria's Golden Jubilee service in Westminster
Abbey. The Queen is sitting on a dais at the centre of
the painting

To emphasise the point about the country and monarchy being united by the ties of family, Victoria announced that she would wear her usual widow's dress and bonnet, albeit decorated with diamonds, rather than her state robes and crown. Moreover, while this would be the largest ever gathering of royal houses, the biggest celebration of all was to take place in Hyde Park, where 20,000 underprivileged children would be entertained with tea and cakes (Fig. 132).

At 11.30am on 21 June 1887 the Queen and her extended family set off from Buckingham Palace in a long line of carriages (Figs 133 and 134). Millions of cheering subjects lined the route to Westminster Abbey, where 9,000 guests, led by all the crowned heads of Europe, had been squeezed into specially built galleries. Unlike the chaos of her coronation, the thanksgiving service went exactly as Victoria had planned (Fig. 135). But, 'oh!' she wrote, 'without my beloved Husband (for whom this would have been such a proud day!)'.

LEFT
Fig. 136
Queen Victoria seated in the Green Drawing Room at Windsor Castle, surrounded by members of her extended family. The painting was commissioned by the Queen to commemorate the gathering of the family for her Golden Jubilee in 1887

ABOVE
Fig. 137
The frontispiece from Queen Victoria's Jubilee autograph book, which contains the signatures of visiting royalty, members of the Royal Household and others involved with the celebration of her Golden Jubilee

The Queen returned to Buckingham Palace for a late luncheon at 4pm. Speeches were given and presents exchanged. At the end of the day, much exhausted, Victoria slipped away from the company to the Chinese Room in the east wing to watch the fireworks by herself. She concluded her journal entry on a truly happy note: 'this never to be forgotten day will always leave the most gratifying and heart stirring memories behind' (Figs 136 and 137).

The Buckingham Palace garden party took place on 29 June. 'I joined all my family (which is legion!)', she wrote, 'and the enormous number of foreign guests, beginning with the 4 Kings who were all there.' (Fig. 138) Buoyed by the outpouring of goodwill towards her, Victoria entered into the spirit of the event with an enthusiasm that had been wholly absent in past years. She walked the entire length of the lawn in front of the Palace, 'and bowed right & left, talking to as many as I could.' After tea she continued her slow perambulation, giving as many people as possible the opportunity to see her.

The Queen participated in more public events during 1887 than she had in all the years put together since Prince Albert's death. Nothing would ever fully assuage her grief at his loss. But she had come to realise that the monarchy was greater than any single person. It existed on several levels: as an institution, as an idea and in the relationship between the Sovereign and the people. The one constant in all three was Buckingham Palace, the place she once described as 'the saddest of [my] sad houses'. What had been impossible for her in 1863 seemed only natural in 1893 when the newly married George, Duke of York, and Princess Mary of Teck, the future King George V and Queen Mary, stepped out onto the balcony of Buckingham Palace to acknowledge the cheers of thousands of well-wishers (Fig. 139).

Victoria celebrated her Diamond Jubilee in 1897 (Figs 140 and 141). This was purely a 'family' affair attended only by representatives from all the corners of the British Empire. By now this encompassed 11 million square miles and numbered some 372 million people. The Times set the tone on the day of the Jubilee: 'To-day the eyes of the whole Empire ... will be fixed upon one who, in a period of all-embracing change has offered during all these years an extraordinary instance of political and moral stability.'

Fig. 138
Queen Victoria, with the Prince of Wales to her right, receiving guests at the Golden Jubilee garden party, held in the gardens of Buckingham Palace on 29 June 1887

Fig. 139
Queen Victoria and the royal family on the balcony of
Buckingham Palace following the wedding of George,
Duke of York, and Princess Mary of Teck at the Chapel Royal,
St James's Palace, on 6 July 1893

Fig. 140
Queen Victoria arriving at St Paul's Cathedral
for her Diamond Jubilee thanksgiving service,
held on 22 June 1897

Fig. 141
The Queen sat in her open carriage
outside St Paul's while the service was
held in celebration of her Diamond Jubilee

The change was symbolised by the use of the telegraph to convey the Queen's Jubilee message. At 11am Victoria pressed an electric button at the Palace which relayed a telegram to the furthest reaches of the Empire. It read: 'From my heart I thank my beloved people. May God bless them.' The other great innovation was the capturing of parts of the Diamond Jubilee on film, showing Queen Victoria in her carriage as she was driven to and from St Paul's Cathedral.

Queen Victoria died on 22 January 1901 at Osborne House at the age of 81. She had reigned for 63 years, seven months and two days. Her body was conveyed to London on 1 February. The procession began at Victoria station, with the Queen's coffin being laid on a specially adapted gun carriage pulled by the same cream horses that had been used at her Diamond Jubilee. Her funeral was held in St George's Chapel at Windsor Castle on 2 February (Figs 142 and 143), and two days later Victoria was laid to rest next to Albert in the Mausoleum at Frogmore in the Home Park, Windsor (Figs 144 and 145). As life resumed in London, Buckingham Palace, one of Victoria's greatest legacies to the nation, awaited its new occupants.

LEFT
Fig. 142
Queen Victoria's funeral procession passing along the High Street, Windsor, before it reached St George's Chapel, where her funeral was held on 2 February 1901

RIGHT
Fig. 143
Queen Victoria's funeral procession crossing the Quadrangle in Windsor Castle, on its way to the Mausoleum at Frogmore

Fig. 144
Plans for the Mausoleum at Frogmore
began in the days following Prince Albert's
death in 1861. This drawing of the front of
the building was made by Queen Victoria
in 1865 and is inscribed 'Our Mausoleum'

Fig. 145
Watercolour depicting the interior
decoration of the Mausoleum.
Queen Victoria is shown kneeling
beside Prince Albert's effigy

Illustrations

Fig. 34
Attributed to Mary Thornycroft
Marble sculpture of Prince Alfred's left arm
1845
RCIN 34581

Fig. 35
Abraham Kent
Marble sculpture of Victoria,
Princess Royal's left foot
1843
RCIN 42016

Fig. 36
Unknown maker
Casket containing the teeth
of Queen Victoria's children
c.1860
RCIN 52617

Fig. 37
Francis Holl after Sir Edwin Landseer
*Prince Albert with Victoria,
Princess Royal, in 1841*
RCIN 605866

Fig. 38
William Gibbs Rogers
Cradle
1850
RCIN 1516

Fig. 39
Invoice for toys and books
purchased for the royal nursery
1847
RA VIC/MAIN/Z/262/127

Fig. 40
Queen Victoria
A sketch of Princess Beatrice and her nurse
28 March 1858
RCIN 980024.ew

Fig. 41
After William Kilburn
*The first six children of
Queen Victoria and Prince Albert*
May 1848
RCIN 2900001

Fig. 42
Leonida Caldesi
Princess Beatrice and Mary Ann Thurston
c.1880 after an original of May 1858
RCIN 2900134

Fig. 43
Guglielmo Faija after
Franz Xaver Winterhalter
Sir Robert Peel
1850
RCIN 420812

Fig. 44
Charles Moore
Brighton Pavilion
c.1830
RCIN 918154

Fig. 45
Hills & Saunders
*The Princesses' Bed Room,
Buckingham Palace*
1873
RCIN 2101759

Fig. 46
James Roberts
*The Pavilion Breakfast Room
at Buckingham Palace*
1850
RCIN 919918

Fig. 47
Franz Xaver Winterhalter
Prince Arthur
1853
RCIN 401032

Fig. 48
Roger Fenton
Buckingham Palace
c.1858
RCIN 2935164

Fig. 49
Joseph Nash
*Queen Victoria's Birthday Table
at Buckingham Palace*
1846
RCIN 919923

Fig. 50
Leonida Caldesi
*Prince Arthur and Prince Leopold in the
costume of the sons of King Henry IV*
7 April 1859
RCIN 2914286

Fig. 51
Leonida Caldesi
*Princess Louise and Princess Helena in the
Swiss costume they wore at the Fancy Ball*
7 April 1859
RCIN 2914284

Fig. 52
Eugenio Agneni
*The Children's Fancy Ball
at Buckingham Palace*
1859
RCIN 919909

Fig. 53
Unknown photographer
*The Prince Consort's Library,
Buckingham Palace*
1865–70
RCIN 2103807

Fig. 54
Hills & Saunders
*The Prince Consort's Organ Room,
Buckingham Palace*
1873
RCIN 2101748

Fig. 55
Roger Fenton
*The Queen, The Prince
and eight Royal children*
22 May 1854
RCIN 2906086

Fig. 56
Queen Victoria
*A watercolour of the view from
a window at Buckingham Palace*
3 June 1853
RCIN 981313.bc

Fig. 57
Leonida Caldesi
*Princess Beatrice taking her
first ride on her second birthday*
c.1880 after an original
of 14 April 1859
RCIN 2900172

Fig. 58
Dr Ernst Becker
*The Prince of Wales and Prince Alfred
with their companions*
June 1854
RCIN 2800675

Fig. 59
Donkey barouche
RCIN 77037

Fig. 60
Samuel Dunkinfield Swarbreck
*A view of the Garden Pavilion in the
grounds of Buckingham Palace*
1847
RCIN 933137

Figs 61 and 62
Ludwig Grüner
*Designs for the decoration of the
Garden pavilion at Buckingham Palace*
1845
RCIN 708005

Entertaining
at Buckingham Palace

Title image
Louis Haghe
*The Banquet for Prince Leopold's
Christening, 28 June 1853*
1853
RCIN 919917

Fig. 63
E. Walker
Buckingham Palace
1852
RCIN 702796

Fig. 64
Eugène Lami
*The Grand Staircase
at Buckingham Palace*
1848
RCIN 919902

Fig. 65
Franz Xaver Winterhalter
Luigi Lablache
1852
RCIN 404692

Fig. 66
? Charles F. Bielefeld
Music stand
c.1840
RCIN 20558

Fig. 67
S. & P. Erard
Grand piano
1856
RCIN 2426

Fig. 68
Queen Victoria
A drawing of Jenny Lind as Maria
June 1847
RCIN 980011.ai

Fig. 69
Ernst Friedrich August Rietschel
Felix Mendelssohn-Bartholdy
c.1849
RCIN 69006

Fig. 70
G. Durand
*Prince Albert Plays for
The Queen & The Composer*
© Mansell/The LIFE Picture
Collection/Getty Images

Resurgence

First published 2019 by Royal Collection Trust
York House
St James's Palace
London SW1A 1BQ

Reprinted 2019

Royal Collection Trust is grateful for
permission to reproduce the following:

Fig. 70: © Mansell/The LIFE Picture Collection/
Getty Images
Fig. 122: Private collection (courtesy of
Look and Learn/Illustrated Papers Collection/
Bridgeman Images)

ISBN 978 1 909741 67 6

101928

More information on the Royal Collection
works featured in this book can be found at
www.rct.uk, by searching on the RCIN numbers
included in the list of illustrations.

British Library Cataloguing
in Publication Data:
A catalogue record for this book
is available from the British Library.

Designer Kathrin Jacobsen
Production manager Sarah Tucker
Project manager Georgina Seage
Colour reproduction by Pureprint Group
Printed and bound in the
United Kingdom by Pureprint Group

Typeset in Hermann and Ideal Sans
and printed on Amadeus Silk 150gsm

Frontispiece:
*Queen Victoria's Birthday Table at
Buckingham Palace*; watercolour by
Joseph Nash, 1846 (RCIN 919923)

Endpapers:
Detail from *The view from a window
at Buckingham Palace*; watercolour by
Queen Victoria, 3 June 1853 (RCIN 981313.bc)